CHRISTMAS FIRST PERSONS
SHARING THE STORY CREATIVELY

BY

ROGER D. HABER

Published by GreatCloud publications

ISBN-13: 978-1540778055
ISBN-10:1540778053

DEDICATION PAGE

To Nanci—who always checked my costumes
on Christmas Eve—except one time!

To my two sons—Timothy and Jeremy—who both
played
Tiny Tim to my Scrooge

To Landon and Jameson—my two grandsons—I hope
one day you'll be my Tiny Tims!

PREFACE

Christmas First Persons. This started when I realized that Christmas Eve services were attended by people who really didn't want to sit through a sermon.

Many people who come on Christmas Eve are dragged there by a relative and come expecting to be bored out of their pew! I wanted to present the Gospel in a creative way. So… Christmas First Persons.

This book can be used by pastors who want to share the Gospel message to their congregations. Other church leaders—youth, children—who want to share the story of Jesus' birth and the salvation he brings can use these dramatic presentations as well.

Some of these Christmas First Persons can be presented by either a man or a woman. Some of these presentations are designed specifically for either a male or female presenter. That will be obvious to you as you go through the presentations.

At the beginning of each presentation you will note some suggestions for costumes and other props you might want to use.

Feel free to adapt these presentations. Use them at your Christmas Eve Service or for an outreach event during the Christmas season.

Would you do me one favor? Let me know how it worked for you. Email me at doctoroger@gmail.com. Thanks.

CHRISTMAS FIRST PERSONS
SHARING THE STORY CREATIVELY

One

The Shepherd

Production Notes: Costume: Shepherd's Robe, Headdress, Sandals, Staff.

Good evening! I'm delighted to be with you tonight. I've come a long way and a long time, to share my story with you.

My name is Murray. I am a shepherd. Yes, I'm one of those shepherds, from the fields outside of Bethlehem, over 2,000 years ago!

It was a tough job, being a shepherd. Early each morning, we would get up and lead the sheep from their enclosures, the sheepfold to the spot where they would be pastured that day. It was a different place each day, because, *oy*, could these sheep make the grasslands bare! We would watch them all day long, rain or shine. If one of them wandered off, we would have to find that lost little lamb and bring him back to the fold.

A lamb or sheep away from the fold and the shepherd, would soon be, alright, I'll say it— dead meat!

11

SHARING THE STORY CREATIVELY

We also had to make sure they had plenty of water. Sheep are not the brightest candles in the menorah. They would die without the care of the shepherd. If there were no streams available for our flocks, we would have to dig wells. It was hard work.

Every evening, we would bring the sheep back to their fold, counting them and calling them by name as they entered their fold, making sure none of them were missing.

And that wasn't the end of the day. We would stay with them through the night too, protecting them from the predators—wolves, lions, etc.

Since we weren't far from Jerusalem, our sheep were raised for the Temple sacrifices. Ever since the time of Moses, our people would sacrifice a perfect lamb, without spot or blemish for our sins. At Passover time, in the Spring, it would be one of our perfect lambs that was slain to remind our people how God delivered us from slavery in Egypt. On the night of that first Exodus, our people killed a lamb and put the blood of the lamb on the doorposts so the angel of death would pass over our homes. Because our people followed this command, our firstborn sons were protected.

So you can see, we had an important job there in Bethlehem. Although, we weren't always the most popular people at parties. You see, we spent most of our time out in the fields—tending sheep, feeding sheep, protecting sheep. And how do I put this delicately? Well, sheep don't smell that great—and neither did we! (Wish we had showers in Bethlehem like you do here!)

Well back to that night that brings us all together across time and space. Actually, I was really glad to be out in the fields that night. Bethlehem was mobbed. Roman soldiers were all over the place. People were coming from all over Israel. The Roman Emperor decided to raise our taxes—again—and everyone had to register in their hometowns. So, as I was saying, I was glad to be in the fields that night. It was a lot more peaceful in the fields with a flock of sheep than in the little town of Bethlehem. It was so crowded that there was not one room available in the Bethlehem Holiday Inn.

Well, I was just dozing off when the brightest light I'd ever seen turned the fields outside of Bethlehem as bright as if it were high noon! An angel appeared to me and my fellow shepherds. At first, we thought we were dreaming, but even the sheep got really quiet. I must admit, we were terrified. Dealing with lions, and tigers, and bears… is a lot different than angels.

But do you know what that angel said? The first words out of his mouth were these: "Do not be afraid. I bring you good news of great joy that will be for all people. Today in the town of David a Savior has been born to you; he is the Messiah, the Lord."

Wow! We knew Bethlehem had been famous a thousand years earlier, when its most famous son, David, became king. But it had been a not-so-important town for a long time. But now, the Messiah, the One for whom we had been waiting for centuries had come! You would have thought he would have been born in Jerusalem—in a palace—with servants caring for his every need.

SHARING THE STORY CREATIVELY

But get this, the angel told us that we would find the baby wrapped in strips of cloth and lying in a manger! A manger! Do you know what that is? It's a feeding trough! The Messiah was not born in a palace or in a mansion. He was born in a stable—a cold and dark cave, surrounded by sheep and goats and donkeys.

And get this, not only did we see and hear one angel, but all of a sudden, a whole crew of angels appeared! You never saw such a sight in your life! The sky was filled with these gleaming and beaming angels. This grand heavenly choir started singing: "Glory to God in the highest and on earth peace to those on whom God's favor rests." I'll never forget these words as long as I live.

Well, as suddenly as the angels appeared, they disappeared. So I said to my fellow shepherds, "Boys, Moishe, Herman, Reuben, we need to head into town and see this for ourselves."

Well, we left one of the younger shepherds with the sheep and we ran into downtown Bethlehem. The angel told us we'd find the baby lying in a manger. So we started checking every stable we came upon. Now remember, stables in Bethlehem were caves. We came to the first cave—just a few cows and a donkey. The same with the second cave. Finally, we found a cave with something beside cows and chickens! There was a man and a woman, and yes, a baby lying in the feeding trough.

We were amazed. He looked like any other baby. But we knew, because we believed the angel of the Lord, that this was the Messiah—the One who would set our people free! The father, now what was his name again? Oh yes, Joseph. He told us his name was Jesus. I would remember that name. I couldn't wait for him to free us from the oppressors of Rome!

CHRISTMAS FIRST PERSONS

We told everyone we met about this baby born in a manger.

Years later (I was a really old shepherd by this time), Jesus came into Jerusalem around Passover. I remember, because this was our busiest of seasons, getting lambs to people for their Passover celebrations. By now Jesus was all grown up. After all,

it'd been over thirty years since that night I saw him lying in that manger.

Over the years I heard many stories about him. This Jesus healed the sick—he made the blind see, the deaf hear, and the lame walk. He fed thousands with a few fish and loaves of bread. We even heard he had raised the dead! Surely soon he would free us from Rome.

But then, after his triumphal entry into Jerusalem, where the crowds proclaimed him as king, he was arrested, tried, and sentenced to death. I actually saw him carry his cross through the streets of Jerusalem. I wept. This was to be the Messiah. He was to rescue us from Rome. But no, he died an awful death on that awful bloody cross on a hill outside of Jerusalem. How could this be?

I stood afar off and watched him take his last breath on that cross. I searched out some of his followers. They were lost. They looked like sheep without a shepherd. I was so broken that I decided to stay with them. We were all camped out in this upper room in Jerusalem. The Sunday after his death, while we were all sleeping, some of the women who followed Jesus burst into the room and said, "He is risen!"

Then it came to me. For decades I was raising sheep for the Passover Celebration. Jesus did not come to rescue us from Rome.

Like those Passover Lambs, he gave his life, he poured out his blood so that we might have forgiveness of sins.

But now he was alive again! When I saw him appear in that upper room, he was shining like those angels I had seen thirty years earlier! It was then I knew that he was truly the Lamb of God who takes away the sins of the world.

One.One

The Shepherd's Wife

Production Notes: Costume: Robe, Headdress, Sandals.

Good evening! I'm delighted to be with you tonight. I've come a long way and a long time, to share my story with you.

My name is Miriam. My husband Murray is a shepherd. Yes, he was one of those shepherds from the fields outside of Bethlehem, over 2,000 years ago!

It was a tough job, being a shepherd. Early each morning, Murray and his co-workers would get up and lead the sheep from their enclosures, the sheepfold to the spot where they would be pastured that day. It was a different place each day, because, oy, could these sheep make the grasslands bare! They would watch them all day long, rain or shine. If one of them wandered off, they would have to find that lost little lamb and bring him back to the fold.

A lamb or sheep away from the fold and the shepherd, would soon be, alright, I'll say it… dead meat!

Murray and the other shepherds also had to make sure they had plenty of water. Sheep are not the brightest candles in the menorah. They would die without the care of the shepherd. If there were no streams available for our flocks, the shepherds would have to dig wells. It was hard work.

Every evening, the shepherds would bring the sheep back to their fold, counting them and calling them by name as they entered their fold, making sure none of them were missing.

And that wasn't the end of the day for these shepherds. They would stay with them through the night too, protecting them from the predators—wolves, lions, etc.

Since we didn't live far from Jerusalem, our sheep were raised for the Temple sacrifices. Ever since the time of Moses, our people would sacrifice a perfect lamb, without spot or blemish, for our sins. At Passover time, in the Spring, it would be one of our perfect lambs that was slain to remind our people how God delivered us from slavery in Egypt. On the night of that first Exodus, our people killed a lamb and put the blood of the lamb on the doorposts so the angel of death would pass over our homes. Because our people followed this command, our firstborn sons were protected.

So you can see, our shepherds had an important job there in Bethlehem. Although, my husband and the other shepherds weren't always the most popular people at parties. You see, they spent most of their time out in the fields—tending sheep, feeding sheep, protecting sheep. And how do I put this delicately? Well, sheep don't smell that great—and neither did they! (Wish we had showers in Bethlehem like you do here!)

CHRISTMAS FIRST PERSONS

Well back to that night that brings us all together across time and space. Actually, Murray was really glad to be out in the fields that night. Bethlehem was mobbed. Roman soldiers were all over the place. People were coming from all over Israel. The Roman Emperor decided to raise our taxes—again—and everyone had to register in their hometowns. So, as I was saying, Murray was glad to be in the fields that night. He said it was a lot more peaceful in the fields with a flock of sheep than in the little town of Bethlehem. It was so crowded that there was not one room available in the Bethlehem Holiday Inn.

Well, as Murray tells it, he was just dozing off when the brightest light he'd ever seen turned the fields outside of Bethlehem as bright as if it were high noon. An angel appeared to him and his fellow shepherds. At first, they thought we were dreaming, but even the sheep got really quiet. They were terrified. Dealing with lions, and tigers, and bears... is a lot different than angels.

But do you know what that angel said? Murray said the first words out of his mouth were these: "Do not be afraid. I bring you good news of great joy that will be for all people. Today in the town of David a Savior has been born to you; he is the Messiah, the Lord."

Wow! We knew Bethlehem had been famous a thousand years earlier, when its most famous son, David became king. But it had been a not-so-important town for a long time. But now, the Messiah, the One for whom we had been waiting for centuries had come! You would have thought he would have been born in Jerusalem—in a palace—with servants caring for his every need.

SHARING THE STORY CREATIVELY

But get this, the angel told Murray and the other shepherds that they would find the baby wrapped in strips of cloth and lying in a manger! A manger! Do you know what that is? It's a feeding trough! The Messiah was not born in a palace or in a mansion. He was born in a stable—a cold and dark cave, surrounded by sheep and goats and donkeys.

And get this, not only did Murray and the other shepherds see and hear one angel, but all of a sudden, a whole crew of angels appeared! You never saw such a sight in your life! The sky was filled with these gleaming and beaming angels. This grand heavenly choir started singing: "Glory to God in the highest and on earth peace to those on whom God's favor rests." Murray will never forget those words as long as he lives.

Well, as suddenly as the angels appeared, they disappeared. Murray said to his fellow shepherds, "Boys, Moishe, Herman, Reuben, we need to head into town and see this for ourselves."

Well, they left one of the younger shepherds with the sheep and ran into downtown Bethlehem. The angel told them they'd find the baby lying in a manger. So they started checking every stable we came upon. Now remember, stables in Bethlehem were caves. The shepherds came to the first cave—just a few cows and a donkey. The same with the second cave. Finally, they found a cave with something beside cows and chickens! There was a man and a woman, and yes, a baby lying in the feeding trough.

Murray and his friends were amazed. He looked like any other baby. But they knew, because they believed the angel of the Lord, that this was the Messiah—the One who would set our people free! The father, now what was his name again? Oh yes, Joseph. He told them his name was Jesus. I would remember that name. I couldn't wait for him to free us from the oppressors of Rome!

Murray and the other shepherds told everyone they met about this baby born in a manger.

Years later (Murray and I were really old by this time), Jesus came into Jerusalem around Passover. I remember, because this was our busiest of seasons, getting lambs to people for their Passover celebrations. By now Jesus was all grown up. After all, it'd been over thirty years since that night Murray saw him lying in that manger.

Over the years Murray and I heard many stories about him. This Jesus healed the sick—he made the blind see, the deaf hear, and the lame walk. He fed thousands with a few fish and loaves of bread. We even heard he had raised the dead! Surely soon he would free us from Rome.

But then, after his triumphal entry into Jerusalem, where the crowds proclaimed him as king, he was arrested, tried, and sentenced to death. Murray and I actually saw him carry his cross through the streets of Jerusalem. We both wept. This was to be the Messiah. He was to rescue us from Rome. But no, he died an awful death on that awful bloody cross on a hill outside of Jerusalem. How could this be?

Murray and I stood afar off and watched him take his last breath on that cross. We searched out some of his followers. They were lost. They looked like sheep without a shepherd. We were so broken that we decided to stay with them. We were all camped out in this upper room in Jerusalem. The Sunday after his death, while we were all sleeping, some of the women who followed Jesus burst into the room and said, "He is risen!"

Then it came to me. For decades my husband was raising sheep for the Passover Celebration. Jesus did not come to rescue us from Rome. Like those Passover Lambs, he gave his life, he poured out his blood so that we might have forgiveness of sins.

But now he was alive again! When we saw him appear in that upper room, he was shining like those angels my husband had seen thirty years earlier! It was then we knew that he was truly the Lamb of God who takes away the sins of the world.

Two

The Angel

Production Notes: **Costume: White sweatsuit, white headband.**

No, I'm not a jogger; I'm an angel. No, I'm not kidding, I'm an angel. Where are my robe, my wings, my halo? Relax—this is the 21st Century!

I am an angel. I stand in the presence of God himself. I am his special messenger. Whenever God has good news he wants people to know, he usually sends me! And tonight I'm here to tell you some good news!

Do you remember the story of Daniel in the Lion's Den? Of course you do.

Well, I know him personally! I was sent to him a couple of times to tell him some good news. I told him about the coming of God's special one and that's why I'm here tonight too!

Folks, I want you to know that God had been planning this good news for some time. I'll never forget the day God's heart was broken. He had made this beautiful garden for his creation. He walked with his friends, Adam and Eve, every evening. But one evening, God came down for his nightly walk and Adam and Eve weren't there. As you know, they had disobeyed God and were hiding. God's beautiful creation was ruined. We angels thought God would destroy it. I remember saying, "Chief, do you want me to get Michael and the rest of the troops together?" How surprised I was when I heard him say, "Gabe, (he always called me 'Gabe') I have another plan."

It took a long time (at least for you humans) to see what that plan was. Even we angels didn't know exactly how it would all turn out. Then one day, the Lord looked at me and said, "Gabe, would you wing your way down to Nazareth?" I said, "Sure Lord, anything you say!" "There's a young girl who lives there," he told me. "Her name is Mary. She is engaged to a nice man named Joseph. Joe's a descendant of my friend David, remember him ?" How could I have forgotten! We really had a party up there when he got old Goliath!

"Well," the Lord said, "this girl Mary really pleases me. She loves me and honors me. She has a heart for me."

"What do you want me to tell her?" I asked the Lord. "Tell her I'm pleased with her. Tell her she's going to have a baby. She'll be concerned because she isn't married yet. Tell her not to worry. The boy will not be the son of Joseph, he will be the Son of God!"

Now folks, I better explain this to you; you see this all goes back to what happened in that garden at the beginning of history. Does anyone remember what happened? Right. Adam and Eve had disobeyed God!

CHRISTMAS FIRST PERSONS

They were hiding from God. They had good reason to hide from God. When you humans disobey God, the consequences are terrible. God kicked Adam and Eve out of that garden and disease and death entered the world as a result. The ivy became poisoned, the bees got stingers, and need I say more about the mosquitoes?

You children of Adam and Eve have been paying the price ever since. But remember, it's my job to announce good news. Pay attention, folk. God said he had another plan, remember? That's where Mary came in.

That day in Nazareth, I told her that her son, the Son of God would be the promised one that all her people had been waiting for.

I later went to Joseph. Boy was he upset! His girlfriend was pregnant! One night while he was wondering what to do, the Lord told me to share the good news with him. Joe, I said, Mary hasn't been unfaithful to you. She is carrying the Son of God! Now listen, this is where the really good news comes in. I told Joseph not to worry about the name, it had already been picked out for him. Call him Jesus, I said, for he will save his people from their sins. You see, "Jesus" means "God saves." That's where God's plan comes in.

All of us angels were hovering over Bethlehem the night he was born. You should have heard us singing, "Glory to God in the highest Peace on Earth"… No. Not "Jingle Bells!"

Jesus grew up. He never sinned; he never told a lie, never cheated; never did anything wrong. He obeyed God every moment of every day. You see, Jesus did what Adam and Eve didn't do. Although we were all out over Bethlehem, a few decades later,

God wouldn't let us come down. Jesus had to go the next mile all by himself.

Because of what Adam and Eve had done, death entered creation. Jesus, who never sinned, took Adam and Eve's place. He took their punishment and the punishment of all their children. We angels wanted to soar down to that hill and rescue him from that cross. His Father wouldn't let us. He loved you that much! He loved you so much he turned his back on his Son. If we were allowed to cry in heaven, we would have done so that day.

God's plan was finished. Jesus, who never did anything wrong, died for all those who did. But the story gets better. On the third day, we angels moved the stone from the grave and Jesus walked out of that grave. Death could beat you humans, but it could not whip the Son of God! He is alive!

Do you want to know what Jesus is doing now?

Jesus is getting ready to come again. The next time Jesus comes it won't be as a baby, it will be as a king. Next time, he won't come to a few shepherds, every eye will see him. Next time, a few wise men won't bow down before him, every knee shall bow. Next time he won't be coming to a cross, but he'll be wearing a crown.

You see folks, Christmas is not really about gifts. It's about God's gift to us.

The reason Jesus came was to give people his gift of eternal life. You won't find it under your tree tomorrow. It is available every day of the year. You don't rip paper or untie ribbons to get this precious gift. You just believe that Jesus died for your sins and place your lives in his hands. You agree to follow him all the days of your life.

I just came down to remind you of what Christmas was all about and ask you to spend some time tonight thinking about that. Will you do that?

SHARING THE STORY CREATIVELY

Three

The Innkeeper

Production Notes: **Costume: Robe, headdress, sandals. Set: A hotel reservation desk with a bell on it. Telephone on the desk (telephone ring sound effect).**

Yes, yes, I can get you more towels... As soon as I can... I'm busy... I'm the only one here tonight. The Inn is packed. This is no holiday for me, that's for sure.

...Oh, I didn't see you come in. Make sure you wipe your feet.

You want a room! You've gotta be kidding. Are you meshuganah? I've been booked for months.

[rrrrrring]

Just a minute, excuse me... Yes, Mrs. Goldberg, I know. The remote control probably needs more batteries.

Now where was I? Now I remember: there's no room here at the Inn.

SHARING THE STORY CREATIVELY

I remember the last time I said that. It was a long time ago, a really long time ago. How could I ever forget?

It was a really long night. People were lined up trying to get a room here. I was in seventh heaven. It was the best business I'd had in years. I was almost glad that the Romans were raising our taxes. Almost, but not quite.

You see, that's why my Inn was in such demand. Caesar Augustus wanted to count all the people in the Roman Empire. This census was to get as many people on the tax roll as possible. Everybody was supposed to go to their hometown and register with the IRS—the Imperial Roman Service!

[rrrring] Mr. Rosen, yes, yes, yes. No. Room service is closed. There's a nice deli around the corner. Yes, their bagels are fresh!

Sorry. This always happens. I'm trying to tell a story and someone needs me. The joys of being an innkeeper.

Well, where was I? Oh, yes, people were coming all over to register with the Roman muck-mucks. The Levines from Bethany were in 103. The Goldsteins from Joppa were in 412. The Portillos (beats me!) were in 349. Well, you get the idea! The place was packed. There was just no room.

I was heading toward the parking lot, about to put the "no vacancy" sign on the door when this couple came in. I'd never forget them. He was a rough and rugged kind of guy. He was a few years older than she. He looked like he worked with his hands. He was very tired. They had traveled a long way, from Nazareth, if I remember correctly.

CHRISTMAS FIRST PERSONS

How could I have forgotten her? She was pregnant—very pregnant! I mean, she was about to celebrate the blessed event right in my lobby. And I just had the carpets cleaned!

It broke my heart. I told them I had no room, not one room vacant in the Inn. As a matter of fact, there was not one room available in the whole town of Bethlehem.

[rrring] Yes, Mrs. Birnbaum. I know it's noisy up there. The Reingolds are having a bar mitzvah party tonight! No I can't move you. There's no room!

Sorry. Well, this couple, very pregnant couple was turning away. How could I let them go? "Think, think!" I said to myself.

Then I remembered. I was almost too embarrassed to tell them, but I did. "Stop!" I said. There is one place you can stay. It isn't much, but it's better than the street.

"We'll take it," they said. "You've got it," I said. "Good," they said. "Let's go," I said. We did.

We went around back. There was a cave there. I used it as a stable for my animals and those of my guests. No pets allowed inside of course!

You had to stoop down real low. It was a bit cramped. This was no presidential suite. I had to shoo out a few goats, lambs, calves, and a couple of chickens, if I remember correctly. (Don't laugh, I'm not getting any younger!)

Well, we brought in some fresh hay. They barely had enough time to get settled when, well, she, well, you know. Alright, already, the baby came!

31

It was a boy! Dark hair, dark eyes, good lungs. Everyone in the Inn knew that! Actually, we realized it for hours that night!

I helped the father clean the baby. We had some disposable diapers in the storage closet. I quick ran and got them. We wrapped him up snugly and placed him in the manger. Oh, you don't know what a manger is. It's a feeding bucket! That's right, a feeding bucket.

Well, next thing you know, some shepherds came running in. Now these guys smelled like shepherds. You know what I mean.

Well, they come into the lobby and say, "Where is he?" "Where's who?"

The Messiah!

Listen, do you think a Messiah would come to my Inn, tonight? Are you kidding me or what?

They said: "Listen Innkeeper. We were out in our fields, watching our sheep. An angel came. He said, 'Do not be afraid. I bring you good news of great joy that will be for all the people. Today in the town of David, a Savior has been born to you; he is Christ the Lord. This will be a sign to you: You will find a baby wrapped in cloths and lying in a manger.'"

Then they told me a whole army of angels appeared in the sky and shouted, "Glory to God in the highest!"

My manger, my manger, my manger—became the receptacle for the Son of God. He left heaven and landed in my stable, in my manger. He should have come to a palace. He should have been laid in a cradle of gold and ivory. He should have appeared to kings, not shepherds.

I might not have had a room for the Son of God that night so long ago. But, I have made room for him in my life. Actually, I've given him not just a room, but all of me.

How about you? Take it from an old innkeeper. The best Christmas gift you can both receive and give is available tonight. You can receive God's wonderful gift of forgiveness and eternal life. You can give him the gift of your life and follow him the rest of your days.

Mary's baby boy is the Savior of the world. Have you any room for Jesus this Christmas?

SHARING THE STORY CREATIVELY

Four

The Real Saint Nicholas

Production Notes: **Costume: Red bishop's robe with white fir trim, bishops mitre, staff.**

Good evening my friends. Some people believe Santa is a fake. Perhaps because they've never met me... the real Saint Nicholas.

You see, the real Santa Claus doesn't live in the North Pole; the real Santa Claus, that is short for Saint Nicholas is from somewhere else.

I don't look like a jolly old elf, do I?

But I am jolly and old. After all I was born in the year 280 during the third century! That means I'm over 1,700 years old! I look pretty good, don't I?

You might be wondering how I got here tonight... Reindeer? Ho, ho, ho. That's the 47th time I've gotten that tonight! You Americans made up most of the stuff about me in the 1800's—the reindeer, the elves, the chimneys! Oh my, you've had some good

---

fun with it, but I'm here to set the record straight. Do you want me to do that?

Well, like I said, I was born over 1,700 years ago in the country of Lycia. That's in what today you call Turkey. I was born in the little town of Patara. Oh my, Patara was a beautiful city on the sea and I loved to travel by ship. My parents were quite wealthy. They were always giving to the poor, but they died when I was nine years old. Their example and love for the Lord Jesus Christ was something I've never forgotten.

After my parents' death, I inherited their fortune. Oh, I suppose I could have spent it on my own needs, but like my parents, and Jesus, I loved to give gifts. I remember this family that lived in our city. The father had been a rich man but had lost all his money. He had three lovely daughters. Each of the daughters was in love with a young man. They wanted to get married, but in those days, a girl had to have money, a "dowry" before a wedding could be announced. The father was very poor. Things got so bad that he was going to sell one girl into slavery so that the others could marry. Well, when I heard about this I knew I had to do something. So I put some gold in a bag, and late at night, I walked to their house. The window was open. I tossed the money into the oldest girl's room and it fell into a stocking that was hung there to dry. Nobody even knew I was there. The father was delighted and the oldest girl had a marvelous wedding. Everyone wondered where the gift came from, but I can sure keep a secret. Well at least I could.

On another night, I did the same thing and so, the second girl got married. She was very happy. Still, nobody knew where the money for the wedding came from. There was one girl left. Well you can guess what I did. I went back with a third bag of money. But this time I wasn't as quiet and the father caught me. He recognized me and thanked me, but I asked him not to tell anyone until after my death. He kept my secret for years!

Do any of you know the symbol that hangs above a pawn shop? Well, I'll tell you, it's three golden balls. They're there because of me. They represent the three sacks of gold I threw in that window. The symbolism speaks of redeeming something of value.

You see my story doesn't really begin with me. It begins with something that happened some three hundred years before my birth. Actually it involves the birth of someone else.

He was born in a stable. In the city of, now what was the name of it again, not only am I old, but I've been dead for centuries. Oh yes, Bethlehem. That was the first Christmas. "Joy to the world! The Lord is come." You see, I learned that this baby Jesus was very special. God saw that people were selfish, proud and cruel. So God came to earth as a baby. Jesus grew up. He showed people how to live and how to obey God. Then he died on a cross so that God could forgive our sins. Joy to the world! That's what Christmas is all about. The Savior is come!

You see, after Jesus rose from the dead, his friends spread the word about him. A man named Paul carried the good news to my country, Lycia. I became a follower of Jesus because the people he told kept spreading the good news.

You see, you and I have value to God. He didn't redeem us with gold at a pawn shop. He redeemed us with the life of his Son.

SHARING THE STORY CREATIVELY

I later became the Bishop of Myra. I spent my life helping people and telling them about Jesus. I was thrown into jail by a wicked king. I represented my country in the First Council of Nicaea where the divinity of Christ was affirmed. The Nicene creed is still recited in many churches today. Your pastor, where is he? Well, he told me that in this church you recite the creed I helped write.

Well I also liberated men, falsely accused who were to be executed. And I traveled all over the known world. But I've never been to the North Pole!!!

Stories were made up about me for hundreds of years. Churches were named after me. In England, they call me Father Christmas; Pére Noel in France. Kris Kringle is what the Pennsylvania Dutch called me and the Dutch called me Sinta Claes. Whatever you call me don't forget that what is really important to me is the Savior I served and followed all my life. Christmas is not about me, it's about Jesus. That's why I loved to give gifts to people because of the gift he had given me.

What is that gift? Well it's the gift of eternal life! The best Christmas gift you can or ever will receive. If my Lord has used me to help you receive that gift, then I will have been able to continue in 21st Century what I began doing in the 3rd Century.

A blessed Christmas to you all!

Four.One

The Real Saint Nicholas
(Woman's Point of View)

Production Notes: **Costume: Greek or Roman style woman's costume.**

Good evening my friends. Some people believe Santa is a fake. Perhaps because they've never met me. I am one of the women whom the real Santa rescued.

You see, the real Santa Claus doesn't live in the North Pole; the real Santa Claus, that is short for Saint Nicholas is from somewhere else.

Now trust me. I knew him. He doesn't look like a jolly old elf.

But he was a jolly man of God. After all he was born in the year 280 during the third century!

He would have loved to be with you tonight but he couldn't make it. No. He doesn't have any reindeer. You Americans made up most of the stuff about me in the 1800's—the reindeer, the elves, the chimneys! Oh my, you've had some good fun with it, but I'm here to set the record straight. Do you want me to do that?

Well, like I said, Nicholas was born over 1,700 years ago in the country of Lycia. That's in what today, you call Turkey. He was born in the little town of Patara. Patara was a beautiful city on the sea and he loved to travel by ship. His parents were quite wealthy. They were always giving to the poor, but they died when Nicholas was nine years old. Their example and love for the Lord Jesus Christ was something he never forgot.

After his parents' death, he inherited their fortune. Oh, I suppose he could have spent it on his own needs, but like his parents, and Jesus, he loved to give gifts. My family lived in the same city where Nicholas lived. My father had been a rich man but had lost all his money. I was one of his three daughters. My two sisters and I were in love. We wanted to get married, but in those days, a girl had to have money, a "dowry" before a wedding could be announced. My father was very poor. Things got so bad that he was going to sell one of us into slavery so that the others could marry. Well, when Nicholas heard about this he knew he had to do something. So he put some gold in a bag, and late at night, he walked to our house. The window was open. Nicholas tossed the money into my older sister's room and it fell into a stocking that was hung there to dry. We didn't know Nicholas was the one who did this at the time. My father was delighted and my older sister had a marvelous wedding. Everyone wondered where the gift came from, but Nicholas knew how to keep a secret. Well, I guess it's no secret now!

On another night, Nicholas did the same thing and so, my other sister got married. She was very happy. Still, nobody knew where the money for the wedding came from. There was one girl left. Can you guess who that was? Right. It was I! Well you can probably guess what Nicholas did. He went back with a third bag of money, but this time he wasn't as quiet and my father caught him. He recognized me and thanked me, but he asked my father not to tell anyone until after his death. My father kept his secret for years!

Do any of you know the symbol that hangs above a pawn shop? Well, I'll tell you, it's three golden balls. They're there because of what Saint Nicholas did. They represent the three sacks of gold he threw in the window of our home. The symbolism speaks of redeeming something of value.

You see my story doesn't really begin with Saint Nicholas. It begins with something that happened some three hundred years before his birth. Actually it involves the birth of someone else.

He was born in a stable. In the city of, now what was the name of it again, not only am I old, but I've been dead for centuries. Oh yes, Bethlehem. That was the first Christmas. "Joy to the world! The Lord is come." You see, Nicholas learned that this baby Jesus was very special. God saw that people were selfish, proud and cruel. So God came to earth as a baby. Jesus grew up. He showed people how to live and how to obey God. Then he died on a cross so that God could forgive our sins. Joy to the world! That's what Christmas is all about. The Savior is come!

You see, after Jesus rose from the dead, his friends spread the word about him. A man named Paul carried the good news to the country where Nicholas lived...Lycia. He became a follower of Jesus because the people he told kept spreading the good news.

SHARING THE STORY CREATIVELY

You see, you and I have value to God. He didn't redeem us with gold at a pawn shop. He redeemed us with the life of his Son.

Nicholas later became the Bishop of Myra. He spent his life helping people and telling them about Jesus. He was thrown into jail by a wicked king. He represented his country in the First Council of Nicaea where the divinity of Christ was affirmed. The Nicene creed is still recited in many churches today. Your pastor, where is he? Well, he told me that in this church you recite the creed Nicholas helped write.

Well he also liberated men, falsely accused who were to be executed. And he traveled all over the known world. But he's never been to the North Pole!

Stories were made up about him for hundreds of years. Churches were named after him. In England, they called him Father Christmas; Pére Noel in France. Kris Kringle is what the Pennsylvania Dutch called him and the Dutch called him Sinta Claes. Whatever you call him, don't forget that what was really important to Nicholas is the Savior he served and followed all his life. Christmas is not about Nicholas, it's about Jesus. That's why he loved to give gifts to people because of the gift Jesus had given him.

What is that gift? Well it's the gift of eternal life! The best Christmas gift you can or ever will receive. If my Lord has used the story of Saint Nicholas to help you receive that gift, then his message from the 3rd Century continues to touch lives in the 21st Century.

A blessed Christmas to you all!

Five

Ebenezer Scrooge

Production Notes: **Costume: Top Hat, Elizabethan English Suit, Cane.**

Oh, good evening. I didn't know anyone came in. Now you're not ghosts are you? Oh, don't get that worried look on your faces, I'm just kidding. That was just a story. I understand people have been listening to my story for many years. Now it is true, I was an awful man. All I lived for was my business. I had no time for my family. I didn't have any friends and I treated my employees like dirt. Why, Bob Cratchit was freezing and I wouldn't even turn up the heat for him. I got a real thrill out of foreclosing on the mortgages I held. My oh my, when a poor widow would come begging for me to give her some more time, I just enjoyed sitting there and then dropping the bomb on her. I would personally go the day my men would throw her out on the street. Often time the furniture wasn't worth very much, but I kept it anyway. I was a terrible old man.

Now most people think I reformed because of some visits from several ghosts. The alleged Ghost of Christmas Past showed me that I was once happy. Well, that much was true. I was once happy.

SHARING THE STORY CREATIVELY

There was a time in my youth when I didn't live for myself. I was even engaged to be married. But then I got a taste of success. And that was the beginning of my downhill slide. Success, making money, power became my obsession. I pushed everyone away from me.

Well, the supposed Ghost of Christmas Present indicated that people were either laughing at me, feeling sorry for me, or hating my guts. While I was counting my profits I was avoiding living life. I didn't even realize it.

The worst was that awful Ghost of Christmas Future, at least that's the way that little Dickens told the story. He showed me my own grave. That wasn't the worst of it. Nobody missed me. People actually were throwing parties and ransacking my house. But that wasn't what hit me the most, again according to the story. It was the fact that my employee's little boy, what was his name again, oh yes, Tim. They called him Tiny Tim. Well, this Tiny Tim was very sick. And of course on the minimum wage I paid Bob, they couldn't afford to send him to a hospital and he had died.

Well, I reformed. I woke up and was a new man. I immediately restored relationships with my family. I visited Bob Cratchet's home and gave them presents, a banquet Christmas dinner and on top of that I gave him a big fat raise. Now you think this all had to do with those ghosts. There weren't any ghosts. I just can't handle pizza after eleven o'clock at night. It was all a bad dream, a dream that made me change my behavior.

But behavior changes aren't enough to have a life of satisfaction and peace. Remember how the story ended. We're all at the Cratchet house and Tiny Tim is so excited that he said, what was that, no, it wasn't "tip toe through the tulips"—oh yes, it was "God bless us all, everyone!"

Well, that got me thinking. Actually, I had never thought before about God. You'd think that I would have been happy. After all, on that memorable Christmas, my family became important to me. I also made some wonderful friends. I made Bob Cratchet president of my company, didn't know that, did you? What did I do? Well, I formed the Tiny Tim Foundation. Not only did I help get that little old Tim back in good shape, I spent all my time helping other sick children whose parents did not have the financial resources. But I learned that doing all these good things didn't earn me a place in God's kingdom. I discovered you can't earn your way into God's heaven.

When Tiny Tim said "God bless us all, everyone," I started a spiritual search. I wasn't even sure I believed in God. But I saw Tim's faith. I was in the hospital and watched the calm peace his parents had as they prayed together while Tim was having surgery. I heard the words their pastor read and prayed in that waiting room. I started praying myself. I said, "God, I'm not even sure you exist, but if you do, will you show yourself to me? If you can fill that hole in my life and give me what I'm missing, let's see what you've got."

Then I started investigating. I discovered Christmas was really about the coming of a Savior. His name was Jesus. He was God himself clothed in flesh. He lived a holy life. He died an awful death for me...and for you! I learned that we deserve to die because of our sin. Now you might not be as bad as I was, but we all deserve to die. But Jesus came to that stable in Bethlehem, not so we could sing "Away in a Manger," but to go to a cross, a cross where he would willingly take our punishment upon him. But that's not the end of the story. On the third day he walked out of his grave! He was no ghost either. He was alive. And because he's alive, he invites people to accept his gift of eternal life, satisfaction and peace. How do I know? Well he invited me and I accepted his invitation. And when I did, my life was really changed, not just on the outside, but on the inside. A joy filled my heart that I had never known, even when I brought those gifts to Bob's house. A peace invaded my spirit that has overwhelmed me ever since. I am now satisfied, satisfied in a way all my money never could provide. All because I accepted his gift, all because I accepted his invitation. How about you? Are you ready to take that step and cross the line tonight and become his child? Or maybe you just want to pray that first prayer I prayed, "I don't even know if you exist, but if you do, show yourself to me." If you do, he will. I know it. Don't be a humbug, make a decision tonight, cross the line or pray the prayer. This will be a wonderful Christmas for you if you remember what Christmas is really all about.

What do you say, Tiny Tim?

"God bless us all, everyone!"

Five.One

Emily Cratchit

Production Notes: **Costume: Elizabethan Dress.**

Oh, good evening. I didn't know anyone came in. Now you're not ghosts are you? Oh, don't get that worried look on your faces, I'm just kidding. That was just a story. I understand people have been listening to my story for many years. My name is Emily Cratchit. You probably heard the story about my husband's employer before. Now it is true, Ebenezer Scrooge was an awful man. All he lived for was his business. He had no time for his family. He didn't have any friends and he treated his employees like dirt. Why, my husband, Bob Cratchit was freezing and he wouldn't even turn up the heat for him. He got a real thrill out of foreclosing on the mortgages he held. My oh my, when a poor widow would come begging him to give her some more time, he enjoyed sitting there and then dropping the bomb on that widow. He would personally go the day his men would throw her out on the street. Often time the furniture wasn't worth very much, but he kept it anyway. He was a terrible old man.

SHARING THE STORY CREATIVELY

Now most people think he reformed because of some visits from several ghosts. The alleged Ghost of Christmas Past showed him that he was once happy. Well, that much was true. He was once happy. There was a time in his youth when he didn't live for himself. He was even engaged to be married. But then he got a taste of success. And that was the beginning of his downhill slide. Success, making money, power became his obsession. He pushed everyone away from him.

Well, the supposed Ghost of Christmas Present indicated that people were either laughing at him, feeling sorry for him, or hating his guts. While he was counting his profits he was avoiding living life. He didn't even realize it.

The worst was that awful Ghost of Christmas Future, at least that's the way that little Dickens told the story. He showed Mr. Scrooge his own grave. That wasn't the worst of it. Nobody missed him. People actually were throwing parties and ransacking his house. But that wasn't what hit him the most, again according to the story. It was the fact that our little boy, Tiny Tim was very sick. And of course on the minimum wage he paid Bob, we couldn't afford to send him to a hospital and he had died—in the dream that is!

Well, he reformed. He woke up and was a new man. Mr. Scrooge immediately restored relationships with his family. He visited our home and gave us presents, a banquet Christmas dinner and on top of that he gave Bob a big fat raise. Now you think this all had to do with those ghosts. There weren't any ghosts. Mr. Scrooge just can't handle pizza after eleven o'clock at night! It was all a bad dream, a dream that made him change his behavior.

But behavior changes aren't enough to have a life of satisfaction and peace. Remember how the story ended. Mr. Scrooge came to our home and Tiny Tim was so excited that he said, what was that, no, it wasn't "tip toe through the tulips"—oh yes, it was "God bless us all, everyone!"

Well, that got him thinking. Actually, Mr. Scrooge had never thought before about God. You'd think that he would have been happy. After all, on that memorable Christmas, his family became important to him. He also made some wonderful friends. He made Bob president of his company, didn't know that, did you? He also formed the Tiny Tim Foundation. Not only did he help get our little Tim back in good shape, he spent all his time helping other sick children whose parents did not have the financial resources. But Mr. Scrooge learned that doing all these good things didn't earn him a place in God's kingdom. Mr. Scrooge discovered you can't earn your way into God's heaven.

When Tiny Tim said "God bless us all, everyone," Mr. Scrooge started a spiritual search. He wasn't even sure he believed in God. But he saw Tim's faith and the faith of our family. He was in the hospital and watched the calm peace that Bob and I had as we prayed together while Tim was having surgery. He heard the words our pastor read and prayed in that waiting room. He started praying himself. He said, "God, I'm not even sure you exist, but if you do, will you show yourself to me? If you can fill that hole in my life and give me what I'm missing, let's see what you've got."

Then Mr. Scrooge started investigating. He discovered Christmas was really about the coming of a Savior. His name was Jesus. He was God himself clothed in flesh. He lived a holy life. He died an awful death for him…and for you! Mr. Scrooge learned that we deserve to die because of our sin. Now you might not be as bad as he was, but we all deserve to die. But Jesus came to that stable in Bethlehem, not so we could sing "Away in a Manger," but to go to a cross, a cross where he would willingly take our punishment upon him. But that's not the end of the story. On the third day he walked out of his grave! He was no ghost either. He was alive. And because he's alive, he invites people to accept his gift of eternal life, satisfaction and peace. How do I know? Well he invited Mr. Scrooge and he accepted his invitation. And when he did, his life was really changed, not just on the outside, but on the inside. A joy filled his heart he had never known, even when he brought those gifts to our house. A peace invaded his spirit that has overwhelmed him all the days of his life. He was satisfied; satisfied in a way all his money never could provide. All because he accepted his gift; all because he accepted his invitation. How about you? Are you ready to take that step and cross the line tonight and become his child? Or maybe you just want to pray that first prayer Mr. Scrooge prayed, "I don't even know if you exist, but if you do, show yourself to me." If you do, he will. I know it. Don't be a humbug, make a decision tonight, cross the line or pray the prayer. This will be a wonderful Christmas for you if you remember what Christmas is really all about.

What do you say, Tiny Tim?

"God bless us all, everyone!"

Six

Simeon

Production Notes: Costume: Robe, Headdress, Sandals, Staff.

I was an old man when I first saw Jesus. He was only eight days old. He was a cute little baby boy. You could tell he was bright by looking into his big, brown eyes. You might be wondering why I was so excited about seeing an eight-day-old baby. You are a very perceptive group for twenty-first century people.

You see, Jesus' parents, what were their names again? Oh, yes, Joseph and Mary—they were godly people. Joseph was a carpenter by trade, but he and Mary knew the Law of God. They knew that Moses instructed the children of Israel to set aside their firstborn sons to the Lord. Wealthy people were required to give silver as a redemption offering—that is to "buy back" their children from the Lord. Since Joseph and Mary were not rich, they offered two young pigeons as the redemption offering. This was what was required of poor people to "redeem" or "buy back" their sons from the Lord! Of course this was also the occasion when Jesus was circumcised too! (But I won't go into that!)

SHARING THE STORY CREATIVELY

Although I was up in years I was still a child of God who loved him with all my heart and walked with him by his grace. I followed the Lord in righteousness and devotion to him because I lived my life in eager expectation that I would see the coming of the Messiah. God's precious Holy Spirit had revealed to me that I would not see death until I had seen him—the Deliverer for whom I was waiting—the Consolation of Israel! You see, it had been prophesied for centuries that the Messiah would come and deliver us from our sins. I was one who believed what Isaiah and the other prophets had written. I was looking every day for the fulfillment of this promise.

One day, as I was eating my breakfast, it was almost as if I heard God's Spirit say to me, "Go to the temple, Simeon, today is the day! Today you will see my Son—the Messiah—the Comfort of Israel. He is the One you have been waiting for—the Great High Priest, the Lamb of God, the Cornerstone of my holy Temple, your Hope of Glory."

So I went to the temple. I sat by the gate and I waited, as I had been waiting all my life. I eagerly looked at other families coming to the temple that day. I saw other parents bringing their sons. When Moishe and Esther came from Hebron, I knew they were not the ones. When Murray and Hannah strolled in from Cana, I was not moved at all. But when the couple from Nazareth came—the carpenter and his young wife—I knew this was the family I had been waiting for.

I don't know what they thought when I reached my hands out to hold their little boy. You'd think they would have run the opposite direction with an old man stretching out his hands toward their precious little infant. Perhaps God's Spirit had spoken to them too, I don't know.

As I held this little child, my heart was immediately filled with praise to God. With joy inexpressible and full of glory, I raised my hands, and shouted to the Lord God:

"Sovereign Lord, as you have promised, you may now dismiss your servant in peace. For my eyes have seen your salvation, which you have prepared in the sight of all nations: a light for revelation to the Gentiles, and the glory of your people Israel."

Mary and Joseph stood there with their mouths wide open. I'm not sure why. I had learned that angels had spoken to them. Why were they so amazed at the prayer of an old man?

I then spoke with Mary. Like the prophets of old, Isaiah, Jeremiah, Zechariah, the Lord gave me a message for her.

I told her that this little boy would cause the falling and rising of many in Israel. There would be those for whom this Jesus would be a stumbling block. Truly many of the religious people would harden their hearts toward this Messiah—this Son of God. Yes, he came to his own, but his own refused to welcome him. But there would be some who would follow him, devote their lives to him and experience his grace, his peace, his deliverance, his forgiveness, and yes, his joy. Many reject Jesus today. But some, even today, once they meet him, follow him.

The road to God's promise is not an easy one. Mary's pain would be like a sword piercing her soul. Yes, she would experience great pain. Following this Messiah brings great joy, but tribulation too. He is Emmanuel—God with us. Because he is with us does not mean all will go well all the time. It does mean it will end well and we will have his presence and his peace all the days of our lives. He truly is the Comfort of his people.

When I exclaimed my praise to God, I also acknowledged that Jesus would not only be the Messiah for Israel but also the light of revelation to those who are not Jewish—I think that includes most of you here tonight (although I understand your pastor is Jewish. Where is he? I hope to meet him before I leave). When I said this little one would be a light of revelation that meant because of his coming, people would have their eyes opened and they would be able to see the way to God. God's message of salvation was to open the eyes of those who were far away—the Gentiles, and to give the glory of his grace to his children, the children of Abraham, Isaac, and Jacob.

I was then ready to meet my Maker. I was ready to depart in peace. With my own eyes I had seen God's salvation in the Person of that little baby—Jesus! Even though I knew I would soon die, my heart was filled with great joy! My role as the watchman for the Messiah was complete. I was ready for the Lord to take me home.

Have you seen him? Are you filled with joy? Have you met him? Will you be ready to depart when your time comes? He knows the thoughts of your very hearts right now. He knows whether or not you sense a need to depend on him tonight and hang your life on him and his promises. He knows now whether or not your heart is going to respond to his call. And one day—all hearts will be revealed before him and his heavenly Father.

CHRISTMAS FIRST PERSONS

Those who respond and welcome him into their lives—who follow him—will experience an eternity of joy and peace in God's presence. Those who reject him, will not experience that kind of eternity, but one of pain, loneliness and eternal fear.

Will you meet him tonight? Will you welcome him tonight? My prayer would be that this Jesus would truly be "...your salvation, which God has prepared in the sight of all nations: a light for revelation to the Gentiles, and the glory of God's people Israel."

SHARING THE STORY CREATIVELY

Six.One

Anna

Production Notes: Costume: Robe, Headdress, Sandals.

I was an old woman when I first saw Jesus. He was only eight days old. He was a cute little baby boy. You could tell he was bright by looking into his big, brown eyes. You might be wondering why I was so excited about seeing an eight-day-old baby. You are a very perceptive group for twenty-first century people.

You see, Jesus' parents, what were their names again? Oh, yes, Joseph and Mary—they were godly people. Joseph was a carpenter by trade, but he and Mary knew the Law of God. They knew that Moses instructed the children of Israel to set aside their firstborn sons to the Lord. Wealthy people were required to give silver as a redemption offering—that is to "buy back" their children from the Lord. Since Joseph and Mary were not rich, they offered two young pigeons as the redemption offering. This was what was required of poor people to "redeem" or "buy back" their sons from the Lord! Of course this was also the occasion when Jesus was circumcised too! (But I won't go into that!)

Although I was up in years I was still a child of God who loved him with all my heart and walked with him by his grace. I followed the Lord in righteousness and devotion to him. I was a prophet. I was only married seven years when my husband died. When I met the little Messiah, I had been a widow for almost eighty years. You see, it had been prophesied for centuries that the Messiah would come and deliver us from our sins. I was one who believed what Isaiah and the other prophets had written. I was looking every day for the fulfillment of this promise.

One day, as I was eating my breakfast, it was almost as if I heard God's Spirit say to me, "Go to the temple, Anna, today is the day! Today you will see my Son—the Messiah—the Comfort of Israel. He is the One you have been waiting for—the Great High Priest, the Lamb of God, the Cornerstone of my holy Temple, your Hope of Glory."

So I went to the temple. I sat by the gate and I waited, as I had been waiting all my life. My friend Simeon was there too. God had promised him he would not die until he saw the Messiah. We eagerly looked at other families coming to the temple that day. We saw other parents bringing their sons. When Moishe and Esther came from Hebron, Simeon and I knew they were not the ones. When Murray and Hannah strolled in from Cana, we were not moved at all. But when the couple from Nazareth came—the carpenter and his young wife—we knew this was the family we had been waiting for.

I don't know what they thought when Simeon reached out his hands to hold their little boy. You'd think they would have run the opposite direction with an old man stretching out his hands toward their precious little infant. Perhaps God's Spirit had spoken to them too, I don't know.

As Simeon held this little child, his heart was immediately filled with praise to God. With joy inexpressible and full of glory, he raised his hands, and shouted to the Lord God:

"Sovereign Lord, as you have promised, you may now dismiss your servant in peace. For my eyes have seen your salvation, which you have prepared in the sight of all nations: a light for revelation to the Gentiles, and the glory of your people Israel."

Mary and Joseph stood there with their mouths wide open. I'm not sure why. I had learned that angels had spoken to them. Why were they so amazed at the prayer of an old man?

Simeon then spoke with Mary. Like the prophets of old, Isaiah, Jeremiah, Zechariah, the Lord gave him a message for her.

He told her that this little boy would cause the falling and rising of many in Israel. There would be those for whom this Jesus would be a stumbling block to be spoken against. Truly many of the religious people would harden their hearts toward this Messiah—this Son of God. Yes, he came to his own, but his own refused to welcome him. But there would be some who would follow him, devote their lives to him and experience his grace, his peace, his deliverance, his forgiveness, and yes, his joy. Many reject Jesus today. But some, even today, once they meet him, follow him.

The road to God's promise is not an easy one. Mary's pain would be like a sword piercing her soul. Yes, she would experience great pain. Following this Messiah brings great joy, but tribulation too. He is Emmanuel—God with us. Because he is with us does not mean all will go well all the time. It does mean it will end well and we will have his presence and his peace all the days of our lives. He truly is the Comfort of his people.

When Simeon exclaimed his praise to God, he also acknowledged that Jesus would not only be the Messiah for Israel but also the light of revelation to those who are not Jewish—I think that includes most of you here tonight. When Simeon said this little one would be a light of revelation that meant because of his coming, people would have their eyes opened and they would be able to see the way to God. God's message of salvation was to open the eyes of those who were far away—the Gentiles, and to give the glory of his grace to his children, the children of Abraham, Isaac, and Jacob.

Simeon was then ready to meet his Maker. He was ready to depart in peace. With his own eyes he had seen God's salvation in the Person of that little baby—Jesus! Even though Simeon knew he would soon die, his heart was filled with great joy! His role as the watchman for the Messiah was complete. He was ready for the Lord to take him home. I was there with Simeon. When I saw the little boy, my heart was filled with joy. I gave thanks to God and I told everyone I met about the redemption—salvation—God would bring through this little Messiah.

Have you seen him? Are you filled with joy? Have you met him? Will you be ready to depart when your time comes? He knows the thoughts of your very hearts right now. He knows whether or not you sense a need to depend on him tonight and hang your life on him and his promises. He knows now whether or not your heart is going to respond to his call. And one day—all hearts will be revealed before him and his heavenly Father.

Those who respond and welcome him into their lives—who follow him—will experience an eternity of joy and peace in God's presence. Those who reject him, will not experience that kind of eternity, but one of pain, loneliness and eternal fear.

Will you meet him tonight? Will you welcome him tonight? My prayer would be that this Jesus would truly be "...your salvation, which God has prepared in the sight of all nations: a light for revelation to the Gentiles, and the glory of God's people Israel."

SHARING THE STORY CREATIVELY

Seven

The Tax Collector

Production Notes: **Costume: Robe, Headdress, Sandals.**

I wasn't the most popular person in Bethlehem. You see, my name is Moishe. I was a tax collector. I worked for the IRS, the Imperial Revenue Service. I'll never forget the money I made that year. I had grown up in Bethlehem. It was a small, but well-known town. David, one of our country's greatest kings came from my hometown. People were expecting one of David's descendants to come from Bethlehem and overthrow the Roman occupation.

Of course, that would have been the end of me, because I worked for the Romans. I was one of their young tax collectors the year that Caesar Augustus decided to take a census of the whole empire, including the people of Israel. Now he wasn't really interested in how many people there were in the empire. His real interest was getting as much tax money as he could for the growing expenses of his empire.

Now back to why I wasn't all that popular. All right, truth be told, I was hated by my fellow Jews. You see a tax collector was seen as one who worked for the enemy. We were regarded as thieves. Remember, the Romans had occupied our land, and I was collecting their taxes. These taxes went to pay the soldiers who forced my people to carry their backpacks for a mile. These taxes paid for the emperor's temples to their pagan gods and goddesses.

Not only that, tax collectors were also hated because of the financial gain we made in our vile profession. You see we were the wealthy people in our community. And that wealth came because we were able to extort much more money than the Roman IRS required. Yes, we collected more than we were required to bring in to the government. I had to buy my tax franchise from the Roman government and I was going to make as much as possible.

Well, I'll never forget that dreary day in Bethlehem when this couple from Nazareth (a city in the northern part of the country) came to register and pay their taxes in their hometown. How could I forget? The young woman was pregnant—very pregnant—about to give birth—I thought the baby would come before the taxes were paid. The husband was a bit older and if I remember correctly, he was a cabinetmaker! I don't think business was going well. They were dressed poorly and didn't seem to be all that happy in paying their taxes (of course, who was happy paying taxes?).

After they paid their taxes, the man asked me, "Sir, can you tell me where the motel is?" This was tough. They had traveled a long way, the wife was pregnant, and I hated to give them the answer. "My friend," I said, "I can tell you where the motel is but it won't do you any good. There is no room, no vacancy, nada! You will not find an empty bed in all of Bethlehem!"

CHRISTMAS FIRST PERSONS

As they walked away, with a discouraged and desperate look on their faces, I felt for this sad couple. Later on I heard that the owner of the motel let them stay in the barn—really a cave behind the building. Can you imagine? A woman giving birth in a barn amongst the livestock, hay, and other accoutrements found in a barn!

As Bethlehem quieted down for the night, as I was counting my profits for the day, I could hear a baby crying. I can remember the shepherds rushing past my house. Rumor has it that some angels came to them and told them that the One we Jews were waiting for, the promised Messiah, had been born in the barn that very night! Could it be? The couple from Nazareth, the couple from whom I collected taxes that very day, was bringing the Anointed Son of David into the world!

The family stayed in Bethlehem for about two years. Every time their taxes were due, Joseph would come and fulfill his obligation on time! But our king, Herod, a Roman puppet, was threatened by the rumor that the King had been born in Bethlehem. He ordered all the boys, two years old and under, to be killed. I will never forget the night when the soldiers came. The wailing and weeping arose from our town like an awful fire!

What would happen to the couple and their son? If he were truly the Messiah, how could he die before accomplishing his mission? The next day, I don't know why, I went looking for them. Their house was empty. Their neighbor said that he understood they were heading to Egypt!

Years later my path again crossed with this one who had been born in Bethlehem on Tax Day! His name was Yeshua ben Joseph! He was building quite a reputation. He taught about loving God and loving your neighbor. He was a lot different from the Pharisees—those men and women who seemed more concerned with keeping commandments than loving God or loving people. This Yeshua didn't avoid or shun us either! As a matter of fact, these self-righteous Pharisees called him a friend of sinners and tax collectors! Can you imagine that?

One day, these Pharisees tried to trap him. They asked him if he thought it was right for the Israeli people to pay their Roman taxes! They knew if he said it was right to pay taxes, the Jewish people, who hated paying their taxes, would ditch him like a bad cold. And they knew if he said it wasn't right to pay Roman taxes, they could have him arrested for insurrection. Yeshua asked for a coin. He asked the Pharisee, "Whose likeness is on the coin?" Of course the Pharisee answered, "Caesar's likeness is on the coin! Everyone knows that!" Yeshua stated, "Then give Caesar what belongs to him and give to God what is His!" This carpenter's son was pretty smart!

As I said, Yeshua was accused of being a friend of tax collectors. It seemed to be true! One of my colleagues was a man named Zaccheus! I heard that Yeshua had a dinner party with this wee little man—a wee little man was he! It must have made an impact on Zack because he became a follower of this great Rabbi Yeshua! He even paid back all the people he cheated as a tax collector, with interest!

Yeshua had twelve men that were part of his teaching and ministry team! One of them was a friend of mine named Levi! One day, Jesus came to his tax booth and said, "Follow me!" Levi left his office and became a member of that team immediately! (I hear

he's writing his memoirs about Jesus under his pen name—
Matthew!)

Of course I heard about his miracles—healing the blind, the
deaf—even raising the dead! I guess even I was getting excited
about thinking of the possibility that he would overthrow Rome
and take his rightful place on David's Throne in Jerusalem!

But then that awful day came! He was arrested! He was tried!
He was sentenced to death! I remember as he carried the heavy
wooden beam of his cross through the streets of Jerusalem. I can
almost hear the pounding of those spikes into his hands and feet
now! I know you won't believe this, coming from a hardened IRS
agent like myself, but I wept! How could this one who was born in
Bethlehem, who did all these miracles, who proclaimed messages
of love and forgiveness die such an awful criminal's death? I
deserved that fate, not Yeshua!

But I soon discovered that something miraculous happened.
My friend, Levi—Matthew, told me that three days later, on an
early Sunday morning, several of the women and other disciples
saw this Yeshua—alive!

I knew that I had to become a follower of this Messiah! I
remember the day I stood in the temple praying. An old self-
righteous "religious" Pharisee stood next to me and proudly
prayed, "Thank you Lord, that I'm not like this wretched tax
collector." I simply stood there, thinking, "I am a wretch." Then I
prayed, "God be merciful to me a sinner." I remember turning
around and seeing Jesus sitting there, watching and listening as I
prayed. I'll never forget his smile. Later on, as I stood there by the
cross. I was with his followers that Easter Sunday morning. I knew
that God was merciful to me a wretched sinner. I soon learned that

he did not come to overthrow the Roman government but to overthrow sin and destruction. He took my punishment so I could receive his righteousness!

I was one of the 500 followers who stood with him on the Mount of Olives when he commissioned us to share this good news of deliverance to everyone we meet. I saw him taken up into heaven in the clouds. I heard the angels tell us that he would one day come again!

If God can rescue this old tax collector—he can also bring you into his precious family of faith! He is coming again! Not as a baby, but as the King of Kings and Lord of Lords! Are you ready?

Seven.One

The Tax Collector's Wife

Production Notes: Costume: Robe, Headdress, Sandals.

He wasn't the most popular person in Bethlehem. You see, my name is Tzipporah, but you can call me Zippy. I was married to a tax collector. He worked for the IRS, the Imperial Revenue Service. Oy, the money he made that year. Both of us had grown up in Bethlehem. It was a small, but well-known town. David, one of our country's greatest kings came from our hometown. People were expecting one of David's descendants to come from Bethlehem and overthrow the Roman occupation.

Of course, that would have been the end of my husband, because he worked for the Romans. Moishe was one of their young tax collectors the year that Caesar Augustus decided to take a census of the whole empire, including the people of Israel. Now he wasn't really interested in how many people there were in the empire. His real interest was getting as much tax money as he could for the growing expenses of his empire.

SHARING THE STORY CREATIVELY

Now back to why my husband wasn't all that popular. Alright, truth be told, he was hated by our fellow Jews. You see a tax collector was seen as one who worked for the enemy. They were regarded as thieves. Remember, the Romans had occupied our land, and he was collecting their taxes. These taxes went to pay the soldiers who forced our people to carry their backpacks for a mile. These taxes paid for the emperor's temples to their pagan gods and goddesses.

Not only that, tax collectors were also hated because of the financial gain they made in their vile profession. You see they were the wealthy people in our community. And that wealth came because they were able to extort much more money than the Roman IRS required. Yes, they collected more than we were required to bring in to the government. Moishe had to buy his tax franchise from the Roman government and he was going to make as much as possible.

Well, I'll never forget that dreary day in Bethlehem when this couple from Nazareth (a city in the northern part of the country) came to register and pay their taxes in their hometown. How could I forget? The young woman was pregnant—very pregnant—about to give birth—I thought the baby would come before the taxes were paid. The husband was a bit older and if I remember correctly, he was a cabinetmaker! I don't think business was going well. They were dressed poorly and didn't seem to be all that happy in paying their taxes (of course, who was happy paying taxes?).

After they paid their taxes, the man asked my husband, "Sir, can you tell me where the motel is?" This was tough. They had traveled a long way, the wife was pregnant, and my husband hated to give them the answer. "My friend," he said, "I can tell you where the motel is but it won't do you any good. There is no room, no vacancy, nada! You will not find an empty bed in all of Bethlehem!"

As they walked away, with a discouraged and desperate look on their faces, and I felt for this sad couple. Later on we heard that the owner of the motel let them stay in the barn—really a cave behind the building. Can you imagine? A woman giving birth in a barn amongst the livestock, hay, and other accoutrements found in a barn!

As Bethlehem quieted down for the night and Moishe was counting his profits for the day, we could hear a baby crying. I can remember the shepherds rushing past our house. Rumor has it that some angels came to them and told them that the One we Jews were waiting for, the promised Messiah, had been born in the barn that very night! Could it be? The couple from Nazareth, the couple from whom Moishe collected taxes that very day, was bringing the Anointed Son of David into the world!

The family stayed in Bethlehem for about two years. Every time their taxes were due, Joseph would come and fulfill his obligation on time! But our king, Herod, a Roman puppet, was threatened by the rumor that the King had been born in Bethlehem. He ordered all the boys, two years old and under, to be killed. I will never forget the night when the soldiers came. The wailing and weeping arose from our town like an awful fire!

What would happen to the couple and their son? If he were truly the Messiah, how could he die before accomplishing his mission? The next day, I don't know why, we went looking for them. Their house was empty. Their neighbor said that he understood they were heading to Egypt!

Years later our paths again crossed with this one who had been born in Bethlehem on Tax Day! His name was Yeshua ben Joseph! He was building quite a reputation. He taught about loving God and loving your neighbor. He was a lot different from the Pharisees—those men and women who seemed more concerned with keeping commandments than loving God or loving people. This Yeshua didn't avoid or shun us either! As a matter of fact, these self-righteous Pharisees called him a friend of sinners and tax collectors! Can you imagine that?

One day, these Pharisees tried to trap him. They asked him if he thought it was right for the Israeli people to pay their Roman taxes! They knew if he said it was right to pay taxes, the Jewish people, who hated paying their taxes, would ditch him like a bad cold. And they knew if he said it wasn't right to pay Roman taxes, they could have him arrested for insurrection. Yeshua asked for a coin. He asked the Pharisee, "Whose likeness is on the coin?" Of course the Pharisee answered, "Caesar's likeness is on the coin! Everyone knows that!" Yeshua stated, "Then give Caesar what belongs to him and give to God what is His!" This carpenter's son was pretty smart!

As I said, Yeshua was accused of being a friend of tax collectors. It seemed to be true! One of my husband's colleagues was a man named Zaccheus! I heard that Yeshua had a dinner party with this wee little man—a wee little man was he! It must have made an impact on Zack because he became a follower of this great Rabbi Yeshua! He even paid back all the people he cheated as a tax collector, with interest!

Yeshua had twelve men that were part of his teaching and ministry team! One of them was a friend of my husband's named Levi! One day, Jesus came to his tax booth and said, "Follow me!" Levi left his office and became a member of that team immediately! (I hear he's writing his memoirs about Jesus under his pen name—Matthew!)

Of course I heard about his miracles—healing the blind, the deaf—even raising the dead! My husband and I were getting excited about thinking of the possibility that he would overthrow Rome and take his rightful place on David's Throne in Jerusalem!

But then that awful day came! He was arrested! He was tried! He was sentenced to death! I remember as he carried the heavy wooden beam of his cross through the streets of Jerusalem. I can almost hear the pounding of those spikes into his hands and feet now! I know you won't believe this, coming from a hardened IRS agent like myself, but I wept! How could this one who was born in Bethlehem, who did all these miracles, who proclaimed messages of love and forgiveness die such an awful criminal's death? I deserved that fate, not Yeshua!

But I soon discovered that something miraculous happened. Our friend, Levi—Matthew, told us that three days later, on an early Sunday morning, several of the women and other disciples saw this Yeshua—alive!

My husband and I knew that we had to become followers of this Messiah! I remember the day my husband stood in the temple courtyard praying. An old self-righteous "religious" Pharisee stood next to him and proudly prayed, "Thank you Lord, that I'm not like this wretched tax collector." He simply stood there, thinking, "I am a wretch." Then he prayed, "God be merciful to me a sinner." He told me how he turned around and saw Jesus sitting there, watching and listening as he prayed. He told me he'd never forget his smile. Later on, we both stood there by the cross. We were with his followers that Easter Sunday morning. We knew that God was merciful to us, wretched sinners. We soon learned that he did not come to overthrow the Roman government but to overthrow sin and destruction. He took our punishment so we could receive his righteousness!

We were part of that group of 500 followers who stood with him on the Mount of Olives when he commissioned us to share this good news of deliverance to everyone we meet. We saw him taken up into heaven in the clouds. We heard the angels tell us that he would one day come again!

If God can rescue this old tax collector, like my husband, and me too—he can also bring you into his precious family of faith! He is coming again! Not as a baby, but as the King of Kings and Lord of Lords! Are you ready?

Eight

Cornelius, the Roman Centurion

Production Notes: Costume: Roman Centurion Costume.

My name is Cornelius. I am a retired Roman centurion. I had risen to my position over the years. My century, the one hundred men under my command, was in the Augustan Cohort. There were six centuries in a cohort. There were ten cohorts in a legion, that is six thousand men.

I'll never forget my first tour of duty as a soldier. I was just a boy at the time when our legion was assigned to the region of Palestine. At that time I didn't think there could be a worse place for me to be. The people of Palestine were not easily subjugated to the Empire. They would not embrace our religious practices. They would not declare our oath of allegiance, "Caesar is Lord." Well, whether they acknowledged it or not, Caesar was in charge. Caesar wanted to know how many people were in the entire empire so he ordered a census. That's when I came on the scene in Palestine. My legion was assigned to the hill-country of Judea. It was a beautiful place. There were rolling green hills. There were sheep grazing on those hills. The place was full of music and singing. I

75

suppose it was then that I first had a taste of the religion, no the faith of these people of God. The people that came to that city where I was stationed, what was the name of that place again? Oh, yes, Bethlehem. They were a proud people. It was our job, not only to make sure the people registered, but also to make sure they behaved orderly. I'll never forget that night when Bethlehem was mobbed. You know how it is, people always waiting until the last minute to pay their taxes!

The first time I heard his name was from the shepherds who were running through the streets that night. They were excited. They talked of angels and singing and of a Messiah born in a stable. I remember telling one of my buddies, "Big deal! What will ever become of a king born in a stable?" What indeed?

Over the years he and I would cross paths. He was different than most of the teachers I heard in Israel. He didn't look down on us or anyone else for that matter. He spoke differently than any other man I had ever heard. He spoke of love and peace and joy. He talked about loving enemies, praying for those who hurt you and blessing those who cursed you. This man really got me thinking.

One day my servant became deathly ill. By this time, I had a great respect for this simple teacher. I had heard that he had power from God to heal the sick. I said to him, "Master, my servant is ill. Say the word and I know he will be restored to me." He offered to come with me, but I knew he didn't need to adjust his schedule for me. I told him that I knew what it was like to be in authority. I knew that all I had to do was give the word and orders would be obeyed. If a Roman centurion could exercise that authority, how much more could this great teacher exercise?

But he was more than a great teacher. I suppose the time I realized it was during those last days of his life. I was an observer and witness to all that took place during those days. I was there standing guard in Pilate's courtyard when they conducted their so-called trial. I was there when they whipped and beat him. I was there when they dragged him through the streets of Jerusalem. I was there when some other soldiers nailed him to the cross. I was there when some of my young subordinates gambled for his clothing. I was there when he was mocked, tortured and struggling. I was there when he said, "Father, forgive them, for they don't realize what they're doing." I was there when he said, "It is finished!" I was there. As I saw the sky get dark in the middle of the afternoon, as I saw graves opened and felt the earthquake, I knelt down on the ground and cried out, "Surely this was the Son of God!"

It was several years before I understood completely why Jesus came. Sure, I tried to live a religious life. I read the Scriptures. I prayed. I was good to my neighbor. But something was missing in my life. One day, one of his followers, a fisherman named Peter came to my house. He told me and my family that the story didn't end with that crucifixion. He told me how on that first Easter Sunday some of the women had met him in the garden outside of an empty tomb.

Yes, he told me that he was alive. Those women ran to him and told him that their Master and Friend could not be kept captive by that hole in the ground.

He's alive!

That day, after hearing Peter tell me about why Jesus came, learning that he died for my sins, understanding that he wanted to forgive my sins and give me a life that meant something, both here and for an unending future, I gave my life to Jesus Christ. No longer would I say, Caesar is Lord. My Lord is now the one I heard about in Bethlehem that night. My Master is the one who taught the words of God those many years ago in Palestine. My Savior is the one I watched die on that hill on that ugly cross. My friend is the one, who from that very cross, said, "You're forgiven."

Ever since I answered his call that day Peter met with me, I have had the opportunity to share the good news with many of my fellow soldiers. There are many of us who are followers of Jesus Christ.

How about you? Maybe you're like I used to be: very religious and a good person. But that's not enough to guarantee an eternity with God. There's only one guarantee, hearing Jesus, the living Christ call you and answering that call, becoming a follower of his. Do you hear the call?

Eight.One

The Roman Centurion's Wife

Production Notes: Costume: Roman Woman's Dress.

My husband's name is Cornelius. He is a retired Roman centurion. He had risen to his position over the years. His century, the one hundred men under his command, was in the Augustan Cohort. There were six centuries in a cohort. There were ten cohorts in a legion, that is six thousand men.

I'll never forget his first tour of duty as a soldier. He was just a boy at the time when our legion was assigned to the region of Palestine. At that time we didn't think there could be a worse place for him to be. The people of Palestine were not easily subjugated to the Empire. They would not embrace our religious practices. They would not declare our oath of allegiance, "Caesar is Lord." Well, whether they acknowledged it or not, Caesar was in charge. Caesar wanted to know how many people were in the entire empire so he ordered a census. That's when Cornelius came on the scene in Palestine. His legion was assigned to the hill-country of Judea. At the time I was in Rome, but he told me it was a beautiful place.

There were rolling green hills. There were sheep grazing on those hills. The place was full of music and singing. I suppose it was

then that he first had a taste of the religion, no the faith of these people of God. The people that came to that city where he was stationed, what was the name of that place again? Oh, yes, Bethlehem. They were a proud people. It was the job of our soldiers, not only to make sure the people registered, but also to make sure they behaved orderly. Bethlehem was mobbed that night. You know how it is, people always waiting until the last minute to pay their taxes!

The first time Cornelius heard his name was from the shepherds who were running through the streets that night. They were excited. They talked of angels and singing and of a Messiah born in a stable. My husband remembers telling one of his buddies, "Big deal! What will ever become of a king born in a stable!" What indeed?

Over the years he and my husband would cross paths. He was different than most of the teachers he had heard in Israel. He didn't look down on the Romans or anyone else for that matter. He spoke differently than any other man he had ever heard. He spoke of love and peace and joy. He talked about loving enemies, praying for those who hurt you and blessing those who cursed you. This man really got my husband thinking.

One day his servant became deathly ill. By this time, Cornelius had a great respect for this simple teacher. He had heard that he had power from God to heal the sick. My husband said to him, "Master, my servant is ill. Say the word and I know he will be restored to me." He offered to come with Cornelius, but he knew he didn't need to adjust his schedule for him. Cornelius told him that he knew what it was like to be in authority. He knew that all he had to do was give the word and his orders would be obeyed. If a Roman centurion could exercise that authority, how much more could this great teacher exercise?

But he was more than a great teacher. Cornelius realized this during those last days of his life. He was an observer and witness to all that took place during those days. He was there standing guard in Pilate's courtyard when they conducted their so-called trial. He was there when they whipped and beat him. He was there when they dragged him through the streets of Jerusalem. He was there when some other soldiers nailed him to the cross. He was there when some of his young subordinates gambled for his clothing. He was there when he was mocked, tortured and struggling. He was there when he said, "Father, forgive them, for they don't realize what they're doing." He was there when he said, "It is finished!" He was there. As he saw the sky get dark in the middle of the afternoon, as he saw graves opened and felt the earthquake, Cornelius knelt down on the ground and cried out, "Surely this was the Son of God!"

It was several years before my husband and I understood completely why Jesus came. Sure, we both tried to live a religious life. We read the Scriptures. We prayed. We were good to our neighbors. But something was missing in our lives. One day, one of his followers, a fisherman named Peter, came to our house. By then our whole family lived in this holy land. Peter told us that the story didn't end with that crucifixion. He told us how on that first Easter Sunday some of the women had met him in the garden outside of an empty tomb.

SHARING THE STORY CREATIVELY

Yes, Peter told us that Jesus was alive. Those women ran to him and told him that their Master and Friend could not be kept captive by that hole in the ground!

He's alive!

That day, after hearing Peter tell us about why Jesus came, learning that he died for our sins, understanding that he wanted to forgive our sins and give us a life that meant something, both here and for an unending future, our whole family gave our lives to Jesus Christ. No longer would we say, Caesar is Lord. Our Lord is now the one my husband heard about in Bethlehem that night. Our Master is the one who taught the words of God those many years ago in Palestine. Our Savior is the one my husband watched die on that hill on that ugly cross. Our friend is the one, who from that very cross, said, "You're forgiven."

Ever since my husband answered his call that day Peter met with him, he has had the opportunity to share the good news with many of his fellow soldiers. There are many of them who are followers of Jesus Christ.

How about you? Maybe you're like my husband used to be: very religious and a good person. But that's not enough to guarantee an eternity with God. There's only one guarantee, hearing Jesus, the living Christ call you and answering that call, becoming a follower of his. Do you hear the call?

Nine

Joseph

Production Notes: **Costume: Robe, Headdress, Sandals. Setting: Workbench with hammer, saw, and other carpenter supplies.**

Oh, I didn't hear you come in. You want to order a what? Oh, yes, I've made quite a few kitchen cabinets in my time. A few thousand years ago, there was quite a demand for them in Nazareth, my hometown.

I was quite well known as a craftsman there. People came from all over Galilee for my woodworking products. I was doing quite well too.

As a matter of fact, I decided it was time to settle down and make a commitment to the family life. Mary and I had seen each other quite a bit. She was a quiet and thoughtful girl. She didn't like to be out front. A lot of people in Nazareth really didn't know much about her, and that's the way she liked it.

People were surprised when I announced our engagement. Joseph ben Jacob is going to marry that quiet little Mary. Mazel tov!

Well things were going well. Wedding plans were progressing. Invitations were being printed. We were all set with the flowers and the caterer. I couldn't wait for Mary to come to my home so we could start a family. I had a dream of a chain of cabinet shops throughout Galilee, and maybe even into Judea. I even had a sign made that I secretly had hidden away—"Cabinet Makers—Joseph and Son."

And then that dream, and all my other dreams came crashing down. I'll never forget the day when Mary came to me with the news that I had never expected to hear—"I'm pregnant!"

How could this be? We were both committed to obeying the Law of our God. We were faithful to each other. I wondered if Mary had been deceiving me all those weeks and months prior to our engagement. Had someone hurt her? What was I going to do? Nazareth was a small town back then. How could my business survive such a scandal?

I wrestled over what to do. According to the Law of Moses, a woman found guilty of adultery would be executed. But I could not even think about that.

I loved Mary. So I decided that the thing to do would be to break the engagement, call off the wedding, and quietly put an end to this so she would have minimal embarrassment.

The night I decided to take this route, I had a dream. A dazzling angel appeared to me in my dream. He addressed me by name, "Joseph, son of David" – you see, I was a distant relative of our country's most famous king—David (don't get excited—I said distant relative—I was a blue collar worker, not royalty.) "Joseph, son of David, stop your plans. Fear not, you can take Mary as your wife. The baby she is carrying has been conceived by God himself—the Holy Spirit! She has not disgraced herself or you! She is actually highly favored by the Lord God. Take her home. She will have a son. Do not name him Jacob after your father. You will call him Jesus, because he will save his people from their sins." (You see, "Jesus" means "God saves!")

I woke up and immediately I went to Mary and said, "We're getting married today!" I took her home and cared for her.

I thought that now life would be easy. Mary would soon head off to Nazareth General Hospital, and we'd have a bouncing baby, Jesus, keeping us up at night very soon.

But good old Emperor Caesar Augustus ruined all that. He decided it was time for a census of the whole Roman Empire. And guess what, the two-donkey town of Nazareth was a part of that Empire. Now you'd think Caesar and all his little Roman lackeys could count us right where we lived. But no, we had to return to our ancestral homes to be counted—and pay the exorbitant Roman taxes too.

Now remember, I am a distant relative of King David. That means my ancestral town is way down south in Judea, in a little town called Bethlehem. Now Bethlehem was so small it made Nazareth seem like New York City (now how did I know that?)!

SHARING THE STORY CREATIVELY

Now picture this—I've got a nine-month pregnant wife and I've got to head way down south to Bethlehem. It's like going from Boston to Hartford!

So we schlep down to Judea and finally arrive in Bethlehem. (Okay, I got lost a couple of times—I can still hear Mary—Joe, let's stop and ask for directions!) After we arrived in Bethlehem, I can still hear Mary's words again: "You didn't make a reservation? You've got to be kidding!

Well, I hadn't made a reservation. After all, we did not have hotel.com in the year zero!

There was no room anywhere. We finally made our last stop at the last inn and the manager said, "Listen, there is no vacancy, but you're welcome to stay out back in the cave I use as a stable!"

Now picture this, I've been traveling with my nine-month pregnant wife for days. And this isn't a joyful trip; we're going to pay taxes! There is no room, no running water, and no cable. We are stuck in a dark, dank cave with sheep. And then Mary goes into labor. And in that not-so-sanitary cave, she gives birth to the Son of God—Jesus. We have no crib, just a manger, and a feeding trough for the sheep. We lay him there.

I look at this baby, so small, so fragile. He is the Messiah for whom our people have waited. He will save us from our sins. Could I really believe all this?

A few hours later some shepherds found us in the stable. "We've come to see the baby?"

"How did you know there'd be a baby in this stable?" I asked.

CHRISTMAS FIRST PERSONS

"An angel told us." Now normally I'd have sent them packing, but since I had seen an angel, I had no problem believing the words of these shepherds. They told me their angel story. The angel had told them, as they were out in the fields caring for their sheep, that in Bethlehem, that very night, the Savior had been born—the Messiah—and they would find him in a manger.

How could I doubt God ever again?

I'll never forget the day we took him to Jerusalem, when he was eight days old to dedicate him to the Lord. An old man Simeon was there. He couldn't wait to hold our baby. He told us the Lord promised to keep him alive until the met the Messiah. Yes, our little baby was the Messiah.

We stayed in Bethlehem a few years. I'll never forget the day that some scientists from Mesopotamia came. They said they were coming to see the king of the Jews. They had followed a star! (I know—a star!)

The only problem was that these wise men told the wicked King Herod about this new king. The old king didn't want a new king. So he was going to murder all the boys of Bethlehem that were born after the star first appeared.

But we had a promise from God—Jesus would save his people from their sins. Again, I had a visit from an angel, and he told me to get out of town. We spent the next few years in Egypt (boy is it hot there!).

After Herod died, we returned to Israel. We went back to Nazareth.

SHARING THE STORY CREATIVELY

When he was twelve years old, we again took him to the temple. Somehow we lost him. Some of you parents know what this is like, right? Well, it gets worse. He was missing for three days. We thought he was with one of his cousins. Where could he be? Someone said he was probably at the movie theater in Jerusalem. We said probably not. Well his mother eventually found him—with the teachers of the law. "Son," she said, "How could you do this to your father and me." We were worried sick!"

Guess what he said. Go ahead, guess. Alright, I'll tell you. He said, "Didn't you know I'd be in my Father's house?" Oy, we were confused. Now I get it.

Jesus helped me with my woodworking business. He'd get the tools, sweep up the sawdust, and he even learned to make a few things. I loved looking at the "Joseph and Son" sign on our shop, but I knew one day I'd have to take it down. I always remembered the words of the angel—you will name him Jesus for he will save his people from their sins.

So, it wasn't much of a surprise when Jesus came to me one day and said he was leaving the family business. Oy, I was upset for a moment. But he was thirty years old. He'd been working for me a long time. The hard thing about losing him was that he never made a mistake. He never cut a board too short. He never said a bad word when he hit his thumb with a hammer. As a matter of fact, he never hit his thumb with a hammer!

Jesus loved being around people. Soon he called a group of people around him. People like Peter and Andrew, James and John, Mary and Martha, to name a few. They were his disciples. They traveled with him talking about God's love. We hardly ever saw him anymore.

Some of you know his story. Not only did he travel around teaching about God's love, but he also healed the sick, cast out demons, fed thousands, walked on water, and knew how to program a DVR—all kinds of miracles!

Some of the people thought he would overthrow Rome and take the throne of his ancestor David! But we knew that wouldn't happen. He came to save his people from their sins.

His mother was so upset the night he was arrested. He was tried—illegally—several times. All of his disciples—his friends— left him. One of those closest to him cursed when his name was mentioned and denied him three times. Another betrayed him earlier that night. He was brought before the Roman governor. He couldn't find anything to charge him with, but for political reasons, he still sentenced him to death.

He carried his cross through the streets of Jerusalem. He gasped with every breath to give hope to a thief, his mother, even forgiveness to those who had nailed him there.

Yes, he came to save his people from their sins.

But the story didn't end when he cried out, "It is finished." On the third day, he rose from the grave—giving hope and joy to those disciples who had forsaken him. He came to save his people from their sins.

The carpenter's son is building something more important now—he's building his eternal Temple with living stones. All those who come to him and accept his gift of forgiveness are adopted into the family of God. Are you ready to come?

SHARING THE STORY CREATIVELY

Ten

Mary

Production Notes: **Costume: Robe, Headdress, Sandals. Setting: Workbench with hammer, saw, and other carpenter supplies.**

Oh, I didn't hear you come in. You're probably wondering what I'm doing at this workbench. You see, my husband was a cabinetmaker. Oh, yes, he'd made quite a few kitchen cabinets in his time. A few thousand years ago, there was quite a demand for them in Nazareth, my hometown.

My husband was quite well known as a craftsman there. People came from all over Galilee for his woodworking products. He was doing quite well too.

As a matter of fact, I decided it was time to settle down and make a commitment to the family life. Joseph and I had seen each other quite a bit. He was quite a bit older than I. He thought I was a quiet and thoughtful girl. He was right. I didn't like to be out front. A lot of people in Nazareth really didn't know much about me, and that's the way I liked it.

SHARING THE STORY CREATIVELY

People were surprised when Joseph announced our engagement. Joseph ben Jacob is going to marry that quiet little Mary. Mazel tov!

Well things were going well. Wedding plans were progressing. Invitations were being printed. We were all set with the flowers and the caterer. I couldn't wait to start a family with Joseph. He had a dream of a chain of cabinet shops throughout Galilee, and maybe even into Judea. He even had a sign made that he secretly had hidden away—"Cabinet Makers—Joseph and Son."

And then that dream, and all his other dreams came crashing down. I'll never forget the day I went to see Joseph with the news that he had never expected to hear—"I'm pregnant!"

Now let me back up a little. I was very young at the time the angel visited me. You can't imagine how shocked I was when he said, "Hey! How are you doing? God is with you and He has a great plan for your life!" Hard to believe, I know! The angel told me not to be afraid. God was with me. I was going to give birth to a son. "Wait a mintue," I thought to myself. "I am a virgin."

The angel said, "Let the Holy Spirit take care of this. You are going to give birth to God's Son. He will be the Messiah. He will reign on David's throne forever and ever." I was so thrilled and humbled by this news that I wrote a song. Do you want to hear a few lines? Okay. "My soul glorifies the Lord and my spirit rejoices in God my Savior." (If you want to read the rest of the lyrics, a guy named Luke somehow got ahold of them—Luke 1:46-55.)

Okay. Back to the story. Remember, I just told Joseph, to whom I was engaged, that I was pregnant.

He wondered, "How could this be?" We were both committed to obeying the Law of our God. We were faithful to each other. He wondered if I had been deceiving him all those weeks and months prior to our engagement. He wondered if someone had hurt me What was he going to do? Nazareth was a small town back then. How could his business survive such a scandal?

He wrestled over what to do. According to the Law of Moses, a woman found guilty of adultery would be executed. But he could not even think about that.

Joseph loved me. So he decided that the thing to do would be to break the engagement, call off the wedding, and quietly put an end to this so I would have minimal embarrassment.

The night he decided to take this route, he had a dream. A dazzling angel appeared to him in his dream. He addressed my future husband by name, "Joseph, son of David" – you see, Joseph was a distant relative of our country's most famous king—David (don't get excited—I said distant relative—he was a blue collar worker, not royalty.) "Joseph, son of David, stop your plans. Fear not, you can take Mary as your wife. The baby she is carrying has been conceived by God himself—the Holy Spirit! She has not disgraced herself or you! She is actually highly favored by the Lord God. Take her home. She will have a son. Do not name him Jacob after your father. You will call him Jesus, because he will save his people from their sins." (You see, "Jesus" means "God saves!")

He woke up and immediately came to me and said, "We're getting married today!" I'll never forget that day he took me home and cared for me.

We thought that now life would be easy. I would soon head off to Nazareth General Hospital, and we'd have a bouncing baby, Jesus, keeping us up at night very soon.

But good old Emperor Caesar Augustus ruined all that. He decided it was time for a census of the whole Roman Empire. And guess what, the two-donkey town of Nazareth was a part of that Empire. Now you'd think Caesar and all his little Roman lackeys could count us right where we lived. But no, we had to return to our ancestral homes to be counted—and pay the exorbitant Roman taxes too.

Now remember, Joseph (and I too) were distant relatives of King David. That means our ancestral town was way down south in Judea, in a little town called Bethlehem. Now Bethlehem was so small it made Nazareth seem like New York City (now how did I know that?)!

Now picture this—I'm a nine-month pregnant woman and I've got to head way down south to Bethlehem. It's like going from Boston to Hartford!

So we schlep down to Judea and finally arrive in Bethlehem. (Okay, Joseph got lost a couple of times—I did say, "Joe, let's stop and ask for directions!") After we arrived in Bethlehem, I had a few more words for him: "You didn't make a reservation? You've got to be kidding!"

Well, Joseph hadn't made a reservation. After all, we did not have hotel.com in the year zero!

CHRISTMAS FIRST PERSONS

There was no room anywhere. We finally made our last stop at the last inn and the manager said, "Listen, there is no vacancy, but you're welcome to stay out back in the cave I use as a stable!"

Now picture this, Joseph has been traveling with a nine-month pregnant wife for days. And this isn't a joyful trip; we're going to pay taxes! There is no room, no running water, and no cable. We are stuck in a dark, dank cave with sheep. And then I go into labor. And in that not-so-sanitary cave, I give birth to the Son of God—Jesus. We have no crib, just a manger, and a feeding trough for the sheep. We lay him there.

I look at this baby, so small, so fragile. He is the Messiah for whom our people have waited. He will save us from our sins. Could I really believe all this?

A few hours later some shepherds found us in the stable. "We've come to see the baby."

"How did you know there'd be a baby in this stable?" Joseph asked.

"An angel told us." Now normally Joseph would have sent them packing, but since we both had seen an angel, he had no problem believing the words of these shepherds. They told us their angel story. The angel had told them, as they were out in the fields caring for their sheep, that in Bethlehem, that very night, the Savior had been born—the Messiah—and they would find him in a manger.

How could we doubt God ever again?

SHARING THE STORY CREATIVELY

I'll never forget the day we took him to Jerusalem, when he was eight days old to dedicate him to the Lord. An old man Simeon was there. He couldn't wait to hold our baby. He told us the Lord promised to keep him alive until he met the Messiah. Yes, our little baby was the Messiah.

We stayed in Bethlehem a few years. I'll never forget the day that some scientists from Mesopotamia came. They said they were coming to see the king of the Jews. They had followed a star! (I know—a star!)

The only problem was that these wise men told the wicked King Herod about this new king. The old king didn't want a new king. So he was going to murder all the boys of Bethlehem that were born after the star first appeared.

But we had a promise from God—Jesus would save his people from their sins. Again, Joseph had a visit from an angel, and he told him to get out of town. We spent the next few years in Egypt (boy is it hot there!).

After Herod died, we returned to Israel. We went back to Nazareth.

When he was twelve years old, we again took him to the temple. Somehow we lost him. Some of you parents know what this is like, right? Well, it gets worse. He was missing for three days. We thought he was with one of his cousins. Where could he be? Someone said he was probably at the movie theater in Jerusalem. We said probably not. Well I eventually found him—with the teachers of the law. "Son," I said, "How could you do this to your father and me? We were worried sick!"

Guess what he said. Go ahead, guess. Alright, I'll tell you. He said, "Didn't you know I'd be in my Father's house?" Oy, we were confused. Now I get it.

Jesus helped Joseph with his woodworking business. He'd get the tools, sweep up the sawdust, and he even learned to make a few things. I loved looking at the "Joseph and Son" sign on our shop, but I knew one day Joseph would have to take it down. We always remembered the words of the angel to Joseph—you will name him Jesus for he will save his people from their sins.

So, it wasn't much of a surprise when Jesus came to Joseph one day and said he was leaving the family business. Oy, Joseph was upset for a moment. But Jesus was thirty years old. He'd been working for Joseph a long time. The hard thing about losing him was that he never made a mistake. He never cut a board to short. He never said a bad word when he hit his thumb with a hammer. As a matter of fact, he never hit his thumb with a hammer!

Jesus loved being around people. Soon he called a group of people around him. People like Peter and Andrew, James and John, Mary and Martha, to name a few. They were his disciples. They traveled with him talking about God's love. We hardly ever saw him anymore.

Some of you know his story. Not only did he travel around teaching about God's love, but he also healed the sick, cast out demons, fed thousands, walked on water, and knew how to program a DVR—all kinds of miracles.

Some of the people thought he would overthrow Rome and take the throne of his ancestor David! But we knew that wouldn't happen. He came to save his people from their sins.

SHARING THE STORY CREATIVELY

I was so upset the night he was arrested. He was tried— illegally—several times. All of his disciples—his friends—left him. One of those closest to him cursed when his name was mentioned and denied him three times. Another betrayed him earlier that night.

He was brought before the Roman governor. He couldn't find anything to charge him with, but for political reasons, he still sentenced him to death.

He carried his cross through the streets of Jerusalem. He gasped with every breath to give hope to a thief, to me, and even forgiveness to those who had nailed him there.

Yes, he came to save his people from their sins.

But the story didn't end when he cried out, "It is finished."

On the third day, he rose from the grave—giving hope and joy to those disciples who had forsaken him. He came to save his people from their sins.

The carpenter's son is building something more important now—he's building his eternal Temple with living stones. All those who come to him and accept his gift of forgiveness are adopted into the family of God.

Are you ready to come?

Eleven

The Wise Man

Production Notes: **Costume: Robe, Headdress, Sandals. Setting: Gifts wrapped on the stage.**

E=mc2. Oh, I didn't see you come in. My name is Shadrach. I am a wise man! What did you say? "Where are the other two wise men?" What makes you think there were three of us? Don't believe everything you see on a Christmas card or sing in a Christmas carol. First of all, we weren't kings. There's nothing in your Bible that says there were three of us. I know, I know, there were three gifts—gold, frankincense, and myrrh. I'll come back to the gifts later. But for now, haven't any of you ever pitched in for a gift for someone? Hey, gold, frankincense, and myrrh are very expensive.

Well, back to my story. I was a member of a group of men called the Magi. We were a priestly caste in Persia (what you call the country of Iran today). Although we Magi weren't kings, we were advisors to the kings. We were charged with watching the stars and trying to interpret the affairs of history from their movement.

SHARING THE STORY CREATIVELY

Your Bible doesn't say a lot about us. Yes, we were from the East. As I said, I myself was from Persia. People assume there were three of us because of the three gifts. However the Eastern Church taught there were twelve of us.

I remember the day we first saw the star. I said to my friends Gaspar, Melchior, and Balthasar, "Hey, do you see what I see?"

They said, "What do you see?" I said, "A star, a star shining in the sky."

"Big deal, Shadrach. We also see stars." "This is a new star," I said. "Something big is happening west of here."

We had studied the Hebrew Scriptures. We knew the prophecy from the Torah. In your Bible, you would find it in Numbers 24:17: "A star will come out of Jacob; a scepter will rise out of Israel."

I said to my colleagues, "A great king has been born. We need to find him and offer him gifts." The other wise men agreed, and we set out on our long westward journey.

I know you think we were there at the manger with the shepherds, but that is simply not true. Don't believe everything you see on a Christmas card. It took us two years to travel from Persia to Israel. Okay, I know, I should have brought the GPS or at least stopped to ask for directions. Sorry. I thought the camels knew the way.

Well, when we finally arrived in Israel, of course we went to the palace of Jerusalem. Where else would a great king be born? Rather than find a great king, we found a miserable one in that

Jerusalem palace. His name was Herod. You couldn't imagine a worse leader than this man Herod. The emperor appointed him king. Marc Antony took a liking to him and supported him with Roman troops. You can imagine how much that endeared him to the Jewish leaders of Israel. Anyone who opposed him, and believe me there were many, were severely punished. You don't believe me. Well, he had his mother-in-law's son drowned. He was one bad pomegranate.

Cleopatra wasn't a big fan of Herod either. But the emperor was, so Herod's position was solidified, especially after Antony and Cleopatra committed suicide.

To give him credit, he did build a beautiful temple in Jerusalem. Someone during the time wrote, "He who has not seen the Temple of Herod has never seen a beautiful building" (Babylonian Talmud: Baba Bathra 4a).[1]

Well back to my story. We arrived in Jerusalem after about two years of travel. We went to this Herod and asked to see the new king. We told him we had seen his star and that we had come to worship him.

Herod wasn't exactly thrilled at this news. He considered himself the king of the Jews. He really liked that job and wasn't going to hand the crown over to a two-year-old boy. (By now Jesus was a toddler living in Bethlehem—you didn't think he was still in a stable, did you?)

---

[1] Elwell, W. A., & Beitzel, B. J. (1988). In *Baker encyclopedia of the Bible* (p. 966). Grand Rapids, MI: Baker Book House.

SHARING THE STORY CREATIVELY

Again, Herod wasn't happy. He called his religious advisors together and told them to find out where this so-called king might be. They found the answer in the writings of the prophet Micah: "But you, Bethlehem Ephrathah, though you are small among the clans of Judah, out of you will come for me one who will be ruler over Israel, whose origins are from of old, from ancient times" (Micah 5:2).

Well, Herod called our little Magi group in and said, "Listen guys. The little king you're looking for is a few miles from here in Bethlehem. Go find him. Come back. Tell me where he is because I want to worship him too."

Well we trucked off to Bethlehem. We saw the star again. It seemd to be leading us all the way. It seemed to stop over a house on Fourth Street, number 777 if I remember correctly. We saw this beautiful little boy. His parents welcomed us into their little home. We presented our gifts—gold, frankincense, and myrrh. They were very appreciative of the gold. Not so much with the frankincense and myrrh. Mary (she was the mother) said, "You guys are wise men! Do you know appropriate gifts for a two-year-old? How about some blocks? Wouldn't some legos have been a better idea?"

"Maybe Mary," I said. "But your son is someone special. We believe he is the Messiah. Your Hebrew Scriptures have a prophecy. Isaiah wrote, 'And all from Sheba will come, bearing gold and incense and proclaiming the praise of the Lord'" (Isaiah 60:6).

I'm wondering if this was God's idea. Frankincense was used in the sacrifices the priests made in the temple. Could it be that this Messiah would be a priest or maybe even a sacrifice?

Myrrh was used as an anointing oil. Did you know Messiah or Christ means Anointed One?

We didn't understand eveything but we knew this Jesus was anointed by God. That's why our hearts were overjoyed when we saw him. That's why we worshiped him.

We decided to stay at the Bethlehem Holiday Inn before going back to Herod with the great news that we found the king—the Messiah. (Fortunately for us there was room in the inn that night.)

But I had a dream. I'll never forget it. I believe an angel of the Lord spoke to me and said something like this: "Don't go back to Herod. He's bad news. If he found out about this little boy, he would put him to death immediately. Go back east. Take a different route. Don't let Herod catch up with you."

Well, when I got up the next morning I told my fellow wise men, "We can't let Herod know about this little boy." They agreed and we left.

Now of course, that's not the end of the story.

Herod was really ticked off when we didn't come back. Since we didn't come back with the address, he determined to murder every little boy, two years old and under in Bethlehem. I told you he was a wicked man. This fulfilled another Hebrew prophecy from the writings of Jeremiah: This is what the Lord says: "A voice is heard in Ramah, mourning and great weeping, Rachel weeping for her children and refusing to be comforted, because they are no more" (Jeremiah 31:15).

SHARING THE STORY CREATIVELY

But God be praised. He warned Mary's husband, Joseph, to get out of town. I think the gold we gave them came in handy. They were able to travel first class to Egypt and live there until this wicked Herod died. Another prophecy fulfilled: "When Israel was a child, I loved him, and out of Egypt I called my son" (Hosea 11:1).

You see, I soon learned that the stars don't govern events. I no longer look to the stars but to the One who made the stars—the Lord God of heaven and earth.

All of the Hebrew prophecies of this Messiah were true. I am a witness to several of them.

Even though Herod and all that is evil tried to hinder this Messiah from doing what he came to do, God cannot be defeated.

This little boy came back from Egypt and grew up in Nazareth. When he was thirty years old, he left the carpentry business. He recruited a group of followers—men and women who left everything to learn from him. He taught them to love God and love each other. He taught them to love their enemies. He taught them that his kingdom was not of this world. He didn't come to overthrow Rome but to overthrow sin.

I heard he authenticated his kingdom with many signs and wonders. He healed the sick, raised the dead, freed people from evil, fed thousands, walked on water, and calmed the sea. But there was a greater miracle.

One night he was betrayed by one of his followers. He was arrested. He was tried. Even though no one could identify a crime, he was sentenced to death. The one who was anointed as Messiah became the sacrifice for your sins and mine. He himself took the penalty for our rebellion on himself. Yes, he died on the cross for our sins.

But that wasn't the end of the story. Three days later he rose from the dead.

He now invites people like you and me to receive his precious gift—more valuable than gold, frankincense, or myrrh. He offers the gift of forgiveness, mercy, peace, and meaning.

Remember what the Hebrew prophet Joel wrote, "...everyone who calls on the name of the Lord will be saved..." (Joel 2:32).

Have you called on the name of the Lord? He has a precious gift for you tonight. The only gift he wants from you is the gift of your life.

Be a wise man, a wise woman, a wise person, and call on him tonight.

SHARING THE STORY CREATIVELY

Eleven.One

The Wise Man's Wife

Production Notes: **Costume:** **Robe, Headdress, Sandals. Setting: Gifts wrapped on the stage.**

Oh, I didn't see you come in. My name is Vashti. My husband was one of the wise men! What did you say? "One of the three wisemen?" What makes you think there were three of them? Don't believe everything you see on a Christmas card or sing in a Christmas carol. First of all, they weren't kings. There's nothing in your Bible that says there were three of them. I know, I know, there were three gifts—gold, frankincense, and myrrh. I'll come back to the gifts later. But for now, haven't any of you ever pitched in for a gift for someone? Hey, gold, frankincense, and myrrh are very expensive.

Well, back to the story. Shadrach, my husband, was a member of a group of men called the Magi. They were a priestly caste in Persia (what you call the country of Iran today). Although the Magi weren't kings, they were advisors to the kings. They were charged with watching the stars and trying to interpret the affairs of history from their movement.

SHARING THE STORY CREATIVELY

Your Bible doesn't say a lot about them. Yes, they were from the East. As I said, we lived in Persia. People assume there were three of them because of the three gifts. However the Eastern Church taught there were twelve wise men.

I remember the day my husband and the other Magi saw the star. He said to his friends Gaspar, Melchior, and Balthasar, "Hey, do you see what I see?"

They said, "What do you see?"

He said, "A star, a star shining in the sky."

"Big deal, Shadrach. We also see stars," they told him.

"This is a new star," he said. "Something big is happening west of here."

My husband and his colleagues had studied the Hebrew Scriptures. They knew the prophecy from the Torah. In your Bible, you would find it in Numbers 24:17: "A star will come out of Jacob; a scepter will rise out of Israel."

He said to his colleagues, "A great king has been born. We need to find him and offer him gifts."

The other wise men agreed, and they set out on our long westward journey. I said to my husband, "You're going where? How long will you be gone?"

He said, "You don't want to know."

I know you think that the wise men were there at the manger with the shepherds, but that is simply not true. Don't believe everything you see on a Christmas card. It took them two years to travel from Persia to Israel. Well you know men. They should have brought the GPS or at least stopped to ask for directions. They thought the camels knew the way.

Well, when they finally arrived in Israel, they went to the palace of Jerusalem. Where else would a great king be born? Rather than find a great king, they found a miserable one in that Jerusalem palace. His name was Herod. You couldn't imagine a worse leader than this man Herod. The emperor appointed him king. Marc Antony took a liking to him and supported him with Roman troops. You can imagine how much that endeared him to the Jewish leaders of Israel. Anyone who opposed him, and believe me there were many, were severely punished. You don't believe me. Well, he had his mother-in-law's son drowned. He was one bad pomegranate.

Cleopatra wasn't a big fan of Herod either. But the emperor was, so Herod's position was solidified, especially after Antony and Cleopatra committed suicide.

To give him credit, he did build a beautiful temple in Jerusalem. Someone during the time wrote, "He who has not seen the Temple of Herod has never seen a beautiful building" (Babylonian Talmud: Baba Bathra 4a).2

Well back to my story. The Magi arrived in Jerusalem after about two years of travel. They went to this Herod and asked to see

---

[2] Elwell, W. A., & Beitzel, B. J. (1988). In *Baker encyclopedia of the Bible* (p. 966). Grand Rapids, MI: Baker Book House.

the new king. They told him they had seen his star and that they had come to worship him.

Herod wasn't exactly thrilled at this news. He considered himself the king of the Jews. He really liked that job and wasn't going to hand the crown over to a two-year-old boy. (By now Jesus was a toddler living in Bethlehem—you didn't think he was still in a stable, did you?)

Again, Herod wasn't happy. He called his religious advisors together and told them to find out where this so-called king might be. They found the answer in the writings of the prophet Micah: "But you, Bethlehem Ephrathah, though you are small among the clans of Judah, out of you will come for me one who will be ruler over Israel, whose origins are from of old, from ancient times" (Micah 5:2).

Well, Herod called the little Magi group in and said, "Listen guys. The little king you're looking for is a few miles from here in Bethlehem. Go find him. Come back. Tell me where he is because I want to worship him too."

Well they trucked off to Bethlehem. They saw the star again. It seemd to be leading them all the way. It seemed to stop over a house on Fourth Street, number 777 if I remember correctly. They saw this beautiful little boy. His parents welcomed them into their little home. They presented their gifts—gold, frankincense, and myrrh. They were very appreciative of the gold. Not so much with the frankincense and myrrh. Mary (she was the mother) said, "You guys are wise men! Do you know appropriate gifts for a two-year-old? How about some blocks? Wouldn't some legos have been a better idea?"

"Maybe Mary," Shadrach said. "But your son is someone special. We believe he is the Messiah. Your Hebrew Scriptures have a prophecy. Isaiah wrote, 'And all from Sheba will come, bearing gold and incense and proclaiming the praise of the Lord'" (Isaiah 60:6).

I'm wondering if this was God's idea. Frankincense was used in the sacrifices the priests made in the temple. Could it be that this Messiah would be a priest or maybe even a sacrifice?

Myrrh was used as an anointing oil. Did you know Messiah or Christ means Anointed One?

The Magi didn't understand eveything but they knew this Jesus was anointed by God. That's why their hearts were overjoyed when they saw him. That's why they worshiped him.

They decided to stay at the Bethlehem Holiday Inn before going back to Herod with the great news that they had found the king—the Messiah. (Fortunately for them there was room in the inn that night.)

But Shadrach had a dream. He'd never forget it. Shadrach believed an angel of the Lord spoke to him and said something like this: "Don't go back to Herod. He's bad news. If he found out about this little boy, he would put him to death immediately. Go back east. Take a different route. Don't let Herod catch up with you."

Well, when Shadrach got up the next morning he told his fellow wise men, "We can't let Herod know about this little boy." They agreed and they left.

SHARING THE STORY CREATIVELY

Now of course, that's not the end of the story.

Herod was really ticked off when the wise men didn't come back. Since they didn't come back with the address, he determined to murder every little boy, two years old and under in Bethlehem. I told you he was a wicked man. This fulfilled another Hebrew prophecy from the writings of Jeremiah: This is what the Lord says: "A voice is heard in Ramah, mourning and great weeping, Rachel weeping for her children and refusing to be comforted, because they are no more" (Jeremiah 31:15).

But God be praised. He warned Mary's husband, Joseph, to get out of town. I think the gold they gave them came in handy. They were able to travel first class to Egypt and live there until this wicked Herod died. Another prophecy fulfilled: "When Israel was a child, I loved him, and out of Egypt I called my son" (Hosea 11:1).

You see, the Magi soon learned that the stars don't govern events. We no longer look to the stars but to the One who made the stars—the Lord God of heaven and earth.

All of the Hebrew prophecies of this Messiah were true. My husband was a witness to several of them.

Even though Herod and all that is evil tried to hinder this Messiah from doing what he came to do, God cannot be defeated.

This little boy came back from Egypt and grew up in Nazareth. When he was thirty years old, he left the carpentry business. He recruited a group of followers—men and women who left everything to learn from him. He taught them to love God and love each other. He taught them to love their enemies. He taught them that his kingdom was not of this world. He didn't come to overthrow Rome but to overthrow sin.

We heard he authenticated his kingdom with many signs and wonders. He healed the sick, raised the dead, freed people from evil, fed thousands, walked on water, and calmed the sea. But there was a greater miracle.

One night he was betrayed by one of his followers. He was arrested. He was tried. Even though no one could identify a crime, he was sentenced to death. The one who was anointed as Messiah became the sacrifice for your sins and mine. He himself took the penalty for our rebellion on himself. Yes, he died on the cross for our sins.

But that wasn't the end of the story. Three days later he rose from the dead.

He now invites people like you and me to receive his precious gift—more valuable than gold, frankincense, or myrrh. He offers the gift of forgiveness, mercy, peace, and meaning.

Remember what the Hebrew prophet Joel wrote, "…everyone who calls on the name of the Lord will be saved…" (Joel 2:32).

Have you called on the name of the Lord? He has a precious gift for you tonight. The only gift he wants from you is the gift of your life.

Be a wise man, a wise woman, a wise person, and call on him tonight.

SHARING THE STORY CREATIVELY

Postscript

I started sharing these First Person monologues for our church Christmas Eve services years ago. I knew that many people who came to church services on Christmas Eve really didn't want to hear a long sermon. So, I decided to come up with short, creative, and hopefully humorous stories that share the good news of Christmas.

My goal of course, is to encourage people to accept the best Christmas gift of all—a relationship with the Lord Jesus Christ.

If you've never "unwrapped" this gift perhaps you would be willing to accept this gift from God right now.

How do you do that? Well, maybe you'll stop right now and pray a prayer something like this...

Dear Jesus,

Somehow I hear you calling me to follow you. I believe that you, the Son of God, came to this earth centuries ago. I believe you died for my sins. I believe you rose from the dead. I accept your free gift of forgiveness, joy, and eternal life. And I will follow you the rest of my life. Thank you so much. Amen!

Would you do me one more favor? Please email me and let me know that you "unwrapped" this wonderful Christmas gift: doctoroger@gmail.com.

God bless us, everyone!

Made in the USA
Columbia, SC
09 October 2018